the **NO-NONSENSE** guide to

INTERNATIONAL MIGRATION

Peter Stalker

The No-Nonsense Guide to International Migration
Published in Canada by

New Internationalist Publications   and   Between the Lines
401 Richmond Street West   720 Bathurst Street, Suite 404
Studio 393   Toronto, Ontario
Toronto, Ontario   M5S 2R4
M5V 3A8   **www.btlbooks.com**
www.newint.org

First published in the UK by
New Internationalist Publications Ltd
Oxford OX4 1BW

Copyright © Peter Stalker / New Internationalist™ 2001.

Reprinted 2002

Cover photo: Maria Issaias, originally from El Salvador, and her son Aaron,
at a demonstration in Los Angeles challenging discrimination against
immigrants and their children (AP/World Wide Photos).

Design by Ian Nixon, New Internationalist Publications Ltd.
Production editor: Troth Wells.

Printed by TJ International Ltd, Padstow, Cornwall, UK.

National Library of Canada Cataloguing in Publication Data.

Stalker, Peter
      The no-nonsense guide to international migration

(The no-nonsense guides)
Includes index.
ISBN 1-896357-53-9

1. Emigration and immigration--Economic aspects. 2. Emigration and
immigration--Social aspects. 3. Economic development.
I. Title II. Title: International migration. III. Series: No-nonsense guides
(Toronto, Ont.).

JV6035.S68 2001   304.8'2   C2001-901907-6

the **NO-NONSENSE** guide to
INTERNATIONAL
MIGRATION

Peter Stalker

About the author

Peter Stalker is a former co-editor of the **New Internationalist** magazine who now works as a consultant to a number of UN agencies. He has written two books on migration for the International Labour Organization: *The work of strangers: A survey of international labour migration* (1994), and *Workers without frontiers: The impact of globalization on international migration* (2000). His website is at www.pstalker.com.

Acknowledgements

Thanks to Manolo Abella and Philip Martin for their helpful comments.

Other titles in the series

The No-Nonsense Guide to Globalization
The No-Nonsense Guide to Fair Trade
The No-Nonsense Guide to Climate Change
The No-Nonsense Guide to Development
The No-Nonsense Guide to Sexual Diversity
The No-Nonsense Guide to World History
The No-Nonsense Guide to Democracy
The No-Nonsense Guide to Class, Caste & Hierarchies
The No-Nonsense Guide to The Arms Trade

Foreword

I AM DELIGHTED to write this Foreword to what I regard as a very enlightened publication that is attempting to put more sense than heat into the debate about international migration. It is so important that this book is being published as part of the *No-Nonsense Guides* series.

In recent years, international migration has ignited a large debate in the so-called receiving countries where it is assumed migrants benefit materially at the expense of receiver communities. Because this debate is largely taking place in the more affluent industrialized Western democracies, it has focused on the economic problems that migrants from the economically-depressed parts of the world are said to cause. In the circumstances, little attention is paid to the more traditional benefits that cross-cultural migration brings to the receiving communities.

Without glossing over the problems that immigration poses, Peter Stalker presents a balanced view of the difficulties as well as showing the benefits both to receiving countries and to migrant communities. That is as it should be.

As a short book on a highly contentious subject, *International Migration* will prove useful to those who care about the topic because it clarifies the issues involved so thoroughly and presents lucid arguments in a very readable manner.

Contemporary problems seem sometimes to overshadow the immense advantages that migration can provide, and to put things in context this *No-Nonsense Guide* includes a historical perspective, citing the benefits to countries and cultures. Peter Stalker has authoritatively removed the issue of international migration away from the hysteria of the Western media. He offers sound arguments about the enriching qualities of migration, economically as well as culturally, for both the sending and receiving countries.

He gives the reader a clear grasp of the facts with plenty of analysis and information. There are statistics showing the movement in migrants from – and back to – their countries of origin.

The book sorts out who is who and why people migrate in the first place. Differences between settlers, contract workers, professionals, undocumented workers and asylum seekers are carefully explained. It tells us who are refugees and 'traditional' migrants; it details the differences between people who leave on the spur of the moment, in fear of their lives, for political reasons, and those who make a conscious, calculated decision to move in the search for economic benefits. It spells out why a 'foreign-born' person is not necessarily a foreigner, as is widely but incorrectly assumed in the debates.

The types of jobs that migrants typically do in the first instance – the so-called '3-D' (dirty, difficult and dangerous) tasks – are analysed, and to some degree this takes the wind out of the sails of those in the receiving communities who may target immigrants and blame them for their own problems – whether economic or social. Because the debate about migration has been hyped in the Western media as the source of most social problems afflicting the rich world, Peter Stalker's book is a welcome antidote, separating the facts from the myths. Readers of *The No-Nonsense Guide to International Migration* will find answers to most of their questions in this very well researched and highly readable book.

Bona Malwal
Editor of the *Sudan Democratic Gazette*
Oxford, UK.

the **NO-NONSENSE** guide to
INTERNATIONAL MIGRATION

CONTENTS

the **NO-NONSENSE** guide to

INTERNATIONAL MIGRATION

STILL THEY COME – grape-pickers and bricklayers, nannies and schoolteachers, computer programmers and sex workers, these and millions more head for foreign lands in search of work, or higher pay, or just the opportunity to make a better life. Around 150 million people are 'foreign-born', living outside their country of origin, and every year they are joined by two to three million more emigrants. This number also includes 12 million or so refugees, driven from their homes by war, or famine, or persecution.

Bangladeshi laborers fly to construction sites in Malaysia. Desperate Nigerians perch on flimsy craft to cross the treacherous Straits of Gibraltar. Mexican laborers clamber across the walls and fences that mark the long and porous border with the United States.

These 150 million people may only represent 3 per cent of world population. But they generate controversy and debate out of all proportion to their modest numbers, largely because as they travel, migrants expose many of the social and political fault lines – of race, gender, social class, culture and religion – that underlie the seemingly settled terrain of modern nation states. To ask about the rights of immigrants is to reopen many awkward questions. Migrants, for example, typically do many of the '3-D' – dirty, dangerous and difficult jobs – and work for desperately low pay. But why should those who do the least desirable jobs get paid less, when they deserve to get paid more? Migrants also require us to think about international solidarity. Should the accident of being born in France rather than Morocco, say, entitle you to be seven times richer? When French and Moroccans live apart, the question scarcely arises, but once they start to rub shoulders there can be uncomfortable and sometimes violent friction. There are questions too about the duties that a state owes to the people living within its borders. Should the state provide everyone with medical care or education or legal protection, or all the other things that are generally regarded as fundamental human rights – or should it give some groups priority over others?

Immigration brings these issues into sharp relief because it offers a specific group of outsiders who are considered by some to be less deserving, and can be identified as a target for discrimination – accused of stealing jobs, for example, or 'sponging' off welfare states. This *No-Nonsense Guide to International Migration* attempts to clear some of the ground by exploding a few of the migration myths. As later chapters explain, immigrants often create more jobs than they take, are likely to pay more in taxes than they use in welfare, and far from undermining settled nations these new arrivals constantly enrich and fortify the multicultural societies they enter.

My own interest in this subject dates back to a period when I was working for the International Labour Organization. This required me to look at the issue in global terms – to consider migration not just from Europe to North America or Australia, say, or from India to the UK, but also from Bolivia to Argentina, from Mali to Côte d'Ivoire, or from Indonesia to Saudi Arabia. It soon became clear that the same issues emerged repeatedly all over the world. This brief guide has been written from a similarly global perspective, and with a corresponding conviction that people the world over have far more in common than they suspect.

Peter Stalker
Oxford, UK

1 How many immigrants are there?

Despite the scare stories of nations being flooded with immigrants, only around 150 million people now live outside the country of their birth – just 3 per cent of the world's population. Some have settled permanently overseas, while others just stay long enough to accumulate some modest savings before returning to their families. Almost all will enrich the countries they visit.

MIGRATION IS CERTAINLY nothing new. No nation on earth can claim always to have lived in the same place. Adventurous individuals, nomadic groups, conquering armies, and traders of every kind have criss-crossed the globe for centuries. Every nation-state regardless of its claims to ethnic purity is the product of multiple overlapping generations of immigrants. Migrants travel in many different ways and for all sorts of reasons. But they can be classified into roughly five categories:

Settlers – These are people who intend to live permanently in their new country. Most – around one and a half million people each year – head for the main 'countries of settlement', notably the United States, Canada, Australia and Aotearoa/New Zealand. To be accepted as a settler, you need to qualify in some way. There are numerous categories but the main ones are for skilled immigrants, and for those who already have relatives in the country. If you are rich enough you can also buy your way in as a business investor: in Canada, for example, you will be permitted to settle if you can invest around $250,000 and have a minimum net worth of $500,000. The US also adds to the excitement by admitting 55,000 random applicants each year through a visa lottery.

Contract workers – These are admitted to other countries on the understanding that they will stay only a short period. Some are seasonal workers, traveling back and forth between Poland and Germany, say, to pick asparagus, or from Mali to Côte d'Ivoire to cut sugar cane. Others will be on longer-term contracts of a year or more. The largest numbers of contract workers are to be found in the Gulf countries: Kuwait, for example, has around 300,000 foreign maids, mostly from Sri Lanka and India.

Professionals – These include employees of transnational corporations (TNCs) who are moved from one country to another: around 1 per cent of TNC employees in local affiliates are expatriates. But companies also recruit many other foreign professionals. In the United States, for example, companies need to apply for work permits if they want to use immigrants for jobs for which there are no suitable US candidates: in 2000, 420,000 workers held these 'H-1B' visas, half of them working in computer-related industries[1]. All industrial countries have a system of work permits: the United Kingdom for example, issued 45,000 work permits in 1999, mostly for highly skilled people[2].

Undocumented workers – This is the polite term for illegal immigrants. Some have been smuggled in, others are overstaying their tourist visas. The United States has the most illegal immigrants– around 6 million, the majority of whom are from Mexico. Western Europe is thought to have around 3 million. But most of the richer countries have thousands of undocumented workers: of South Korea's quarter of a million foreign workers, for example, more than half are there illegally.

Refugees and asylum seekers – A refugee is defined by the UN as someone who has 'a well-founded fear of persecution for reasons of race, religion, nationality, membership of a particular social group, or political opinion'. But during the 1990s more and more receiving governments started referring to such people as 'asylum seekers' and only termed them 'refugees' when their claims were accepted. This was because immigration officials suspected that many more people were 'economic refugees' who were only claiming asylum because they would not qualify for admission as migrant workers. In cases of mass flight, however, when thousands of people escape across a border fleeing war or famine they are generally still accepted as a group without having to undergo individual vetting. On this basis at the end of 2000 there were around 12 million refugees around the world and 900,000 asylum seekers.

These categories do not exhaust the possibilities; one could, for example, also include long-stay tourists and business visitors as migrants. Moreover, most of these categories overlap to some extent: Indian computer programmers working in Silicon Valley are often both professionals and contract workers; and while most refugees leave for political reasons they have to earn a living in their new countries so may work either as casual or full-time employees.

Sorting out the flows and the stocks

Newspaper headlines about floods of asylum seekers and economic migrants might suggest that international migration is escalating rapidly, and veering out of control. But a closer look at the facts reveals a less dramatic picture. To understand the current situation it is important to distinguish between 'flows' and 'stocks'. Flows are the number of people moving across international frontiers each year, while stocks represent the accumulation of flows – the total number of immigrants living within a country at any given time.

The problem with estimating international flows is that different countries record them in different ways. Some do not gather the information at all: France, for example, records immigrants, but has no systematic way of recording the total number of emigrants, which makes it difficult to estimate net migration. Different countries also make different choices about who to count as immigrants. Thus Sweden excludes asylum seekers from its data on inflows and outflows, while Germany includes them. So comparing and collating data from one country to another is a tricky business.

Flows can be quite volatile, and show considerable swings from year to year. Germany for example had a net outflow of 33,000 people in 1998. That sounds like a modest level of activity but actually represents a substantial movement of people: in 1998, 606,000 came in but 639,000 left, most of whom were asylum seekers and refugees returning home. In 1998 100,000 Bosnians returned. Though there are often dramatic pictures of refugees arriving, there is very little media coverage when they return home.

The figures on stocks are less volatile and are usually more comparable internationally. Again, however, these are gathered in different ways. The most complete and up-to-date information is available in those countries that maintain 'population registers'. In Denmark, for example, each person has an identity number and all the key information on them is regularly updated, with changes of address, say, or whether or not they are married. Other countries shy away from such comprehensive data gathering, regarding it as an invasion of privacy.

One option, as in the United States, is to collect this information in the national census. This gives a fairly good picture of the population as a whole, though it has a number of drawbacks. One is that censuses usually only take place every ten years, so the information is soon out of date. Another is that census enumerators frequently fail to reach people from minority groups, and are even less likely to get a response from anyone who is in the country illegally.

Another option is through surveys of employment. Most countries carry these out regularly in order to monitor economic trends. The UK, for example, has annual 'Labor Force Surveys' that include questions on citizenship and place of birth. These of course only gather information on the people who are working and say nothing about children, or those who have retired. But generally around 70 per cent of the adult population is in the labor force – either working or looking for work – so the labor force survey does give a fairly up-to-date idea of the proportion of immigrants and where they come from.

Who is a foreigner?

One area of confusion when talking about immigrants is deciding who exactly is a foreigner. Here the key distinction is between someone who is 'foreign-born' and someone who has a foreign nationality – that is, who travels on a passport issued by another country. Any immigrant who naturalizes as a citizen of their new country immediately ceases to be a 'foreigner' but he or she will always be foreign-born. According to the US census for 1990, 7.9 per cent of the population were foreign-born, but only 4.7 per cent were still foreigners because the rest had become naturalized citizens. This means that the proportion of foreigners will depend to a certain extent on how easy it is to become a citizen. In France, for example, the proportion of residents who are foreigners has remain fairly stable since 1975, at 6 to 7 per cent , but the proportion who are foreign-born is probably around 11 per cent[3]. In Germany on the other hand, naturalization has traditionally been more difficult so the proportion of foreigners remains higher.

A further complication is that some people regard anyone belonging to an ethnic minority as an immigrant, even if they have been born in that country. In the United Kingdom around 6 per cent of the population belong to a minority ethnic group. The foreign-born however are only 4 per cent, and many of those are 'white' people who have come from Europe, Australia and elsewhere[4].

Globally, the UN estimated in 1965 that there were 75 million people who had been residents in a country

other than that of their birth for more than one year –
that is, they were 'foreign-born born'. By 1975 the
number was up to 84 million, by 1985 it was 105 million, and by 1990 it had reached 120 million. Until the
1980s the number of people who were foreign-born
born was growing more slowly than world population.
But then population growth started to slow while
migration accelerated. The current estimate of 150
million for 2000, comes from the UN's International
Organization for Migration.

Some of the most consistent and up-to-date information on migration is available for the group of rich

**Table 1.1 – Stocks of foreign citizens in selected OECD
countries, 1988 and 1998**

	1988		1998	
	'000s	per cent of pop.	'000s	per cent of pop.
Austria	344	4.5	737	9.1
Belgium	869	8.8	892	8.7
Denmark	142	2.8	256	4.8
Finland	19	0.4	85	1.6
France	3,714	6.8	3,597	6.3
Germany	4,489	7.3	7,320	8.9
Ireland	82	2.4	111	3.0
Italy	645	1.1	1,250	2.1
Japan	941	0.8	1,512	1.2
Luxembourg	106	27.4	153	35.6
Netherlands	624	4.2	662	4.2
Norway	136	3.2	165	3.7
Portugal	95	1.0	178	1.8
Spain	360	0.9	720	1.8
Sweden	421	5.0	500	5.6
Switzerland	1,007	15.2	1,348	19.0
United Kingdom	1,821	3.2	2,207	3.8

Note: This information comes from population registers, except for France
(census), Ireland and the United Kingdom (labor force surveys), Japan and
Switzerland (registers of foreigners) and Italy, Portugal and Spain (issues of
residence permits).

SOPEMI (2000)

Table 1.2 – Stocks of the foreign-born in selected OECD countries, 1991 and 1998

	1991		1998	
	'000s	per cent of pop.	'000s	per cent of pop.
Australia	3,965	22.9	4,394	23.4
Canada	4,343	16.1	4,971	17.4
United States	19,767	7.9	26,300	9.8

Note: This information comes from censuses, except for the United States in 1998 where it comes from a population sample survey.

SOPEMI (2000)

countries that belong to the Organization for Economic Cooperation and Development, which produces the information in tables 1.1 and 1.2, under the French acronym SOPEMI (*Système d'observation permanente des migrations*). Table 1.1 gives the number and proportion of foreign citizens, which is what the countries that do not consider themselves countries of immigration prefer to keep track of. The three main countries of settlement record the numbers of foreign-born which is what appears in table 1.2.

As these tables show, the countries with the highest proportions of foreigners are Luxembourg and Switzerland. In fact in the case of Luxembourg this greatly understates the proportion of foreign workers since a further one-quarter of the labor force commute in each day from France, Belgium or Germany. These international commuters are called *frontaliers*. Switzerland also has a large number of *frontaliers*, many coming into Geneva every day from France. For most countries the number of foreign citizens or foreign-born increased over the period 1988-98. France and Belgium appear to be exceptions, but only because many of their foreign-born born subsequently became citizens.

In most countries the proportion of immigrants is still fairly modest – 3.8 per cent in the United Kingdom. It is also worth noting that for all the hysteria about asylum seekers they in turn represent a tiny proportion of the immigrant population. In mid-2000 in the UK there were around 90,000 asylum seekers awaiting decisions. Not many succeed: between 1988 and 1998 only 58,000 people were given the right to settle[5]. These numbers are very small compared with a total foreign population of 2.2 million.

The best historical records on immigration come from the United States. As figure 1.1 indicates, the flows in recent years, at around 800,000 are still far below the rates of immigration at the beginning of the last century. Moreover the inflows today also represent a much smaller proportion of the total population. In the peak year of 1914 the total number of immigrants was over 1.2 million which was equivalent to 1.5 per cent of the population at that time, whereas the 1998 total of 680,000 was only 0.35 per cent of the population in that year.

So to say that the industrial countries are being

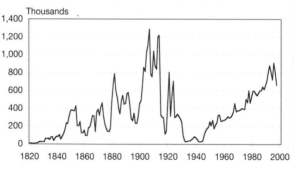

Historic flows

Since the 1960s, the number of people migrating to the United States for settlement has increased – to around 800,000 per year. But this is still far short of the peak years at the beginning of the 20th century, when more than 1.2 million people arrived. Around one-third of official immigrants subsequently emigrate. ∎

Thousands

Figure 1.1 Official immigration to the United States 1820-2000

Immigration and Naturalization Service (various years)

'swamped' with immigrants and asylum seekers is some way off the mark. Compared with the total populations, and with the historical record, the numbers are actually quite modest. Moreover while many new flows of migrants may appear to start, less noticeable is that others tail off. Why people migrate, and stop migrating, is the subject of the following chapter.

1 Migration News (2000). Vol. 7, No. 12, December. **2** SOPEMI (2000). *Trends in International Migration*, Paris. OECD. p. 268. **3** Stalker, P. (1994) *The Work of Strangers*, Geneva, ILO. p 189. **4** UK National Statistics (2001). www.statistics.gov.uk/ukin_figs/Data_population.asp. **5** Travis, Alan (2000). 'Cutting off our nose to spite a race', in *The Guardian*, Feb 17.

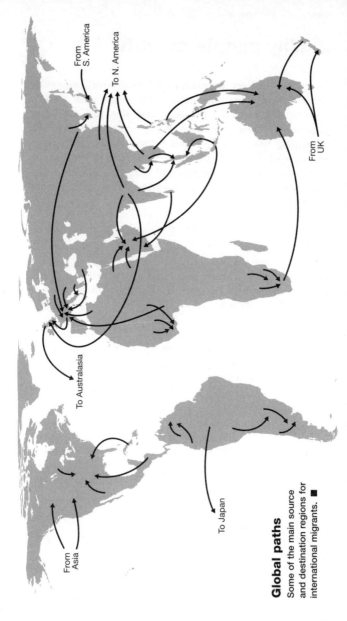

Global paths

Some of the main source and destination regions for international migrants. ◼

From S. America

To N. America

From UK

To Australasia

From Asia

To Japan

2 Why people migrate

Theories that try to explain international migration at their simplest are based on 'push and pull' – chiefly the push of poverty and the pull of labor shortage. There are also more ambitious models, including the grandly titled 'world systems theory'. But one of the most persistent factors is the 'shock of the new' – as modernization and globalization disrupt people's lives and shake them loose into a more fluid world.

MOST PEOPLE MIGRATE from one country to another because they think they will be better off. Some succeed dramatically. In the United States, many first-generation immigrants have arrived virtually penniless and rapidly become multi-millionaires. Sabeer Bhatia, for example, came to the US from India in 1988 with $200 in his pocket. He then invented Hotmail which in 1998 he sold to Microsoft for $10 million. Others have more modest, short-term ambitions: Bangladeshi construction workers in Kuwait just want to stay for a year or two to save a couple of thousand dollars that they can take back home to build a new house or invest in a new business or to pay for their children's education.

Each migrant has his or her own motives for traveling and has a different experience. Nevertheless there are some common features and patterns, and also a few puzzles. Many people certainly want to escape poverty, but not all poor people migrate. Côte d'Ivoire, for example, with a per capita GDP (Gross Domestic Product) of $1,600 is by global standards a poor country yet relatively few of its people leave. Aotearoa/New Zealand on the other hand is one of the world's richest countries, with a GDP per capita of $17,000, yet more people are leaving than arriving. You might think that ease of movement to a neighboring country is an important factor. This would certainly account for the mass migration from Mexico to the United States, for example. But what about the Philippines, which is geographically far more isolated yet is also a prolific generator of emigrants? Perhaps the presence or absence of border controls will shape people's decisions. If so, why do Greek citizens, who are free to live and work anywhere within the European Union, not all flock to Luxembourg where the average per capita income is twice as high?

Theories of migration

There have been numerous theories of migration that could help answer such questions. These boil down to two main approaches: the *individual* and the *structural*. The individual analysis regards each migrant as a rational human being who carefully weighs up the available options, and looks at the destinations that offer the highest wage rates and the best prospects of finding work. This is also called the 'human capital' approach; just as footloose financial capital roams the world seeking the most profitable opportunities, so individual migrants who are endowed with certain educational qualifications, or expertise, or just plain muscle power, will assess where they can get the best returns on the human capital that they embody. A Thai laborer would find, for example, that he might earn more by crossing the border into Malaysia, where the minimum wage is around $100 per month, but he would probably do even better if he invested a few hundred dollars on travel expenses and worked on a collective farm in Israel where the minimum monthly wage is $650.

But migration is not necessarily an individual decision. Often a whole family will plan the strategy, sending one or two people overseas as a way of spreading risks. Few developing countries have any form of social security, so family members try to offer mutual protection. Just as a prudent financial investor will buy a range of different shares, so a prudent family will try to assemble a diverse portfolio of workers. One son or daughter will work on the family farm, say; another might look for a salaried job in the nearest town, while a third could look for work overseas. In this 'co-insurance' system the head of the family will pay the emigrant's travel expenses and living costs while he or she looks for work. The migrant correspondingly promises to send money home, and perhaps to increase the remittances if the family suffers a setback such as a crop failure.

The choice of who to send is often finely balanced. One study in the Philippines weighed up the options for sending family members to Singapore. Although a son working on a construction site might earn more than a daughter working as a maid, the daughter would send remittances more reliably. This household concept of migration is sometimes referred to as the 'New Economics of Migration', though by now it is no longer very novel.

The structuralist approach is rather different. In this view, the migrant is more like a ball in a pinball machine, knocked around by forces beyond his or her control. These forces could be economic, or social, or political – pushing people out of one country and pulling them towards another. In the sending country the structural forces pushing emigrants out could be population pressure, or land shortage, or gender discrimination. In the receiving country the structural forces attracting the immigrant could be a shrinking population, or a shortage of people to work on the land, or the demand for domestic servants. In these circumstances, the daughter of a landless Sri Lankan farmer might find it difficult to resist the forces 'impelling' her to work in Kuwait or Singapore.

The structuralist approach has a number of variants. One is the theory of 'dual labor markets'. This argues that capitalist development does not simply generate a smooth spectrum of jobs from low-skilled to high-skilled – offering employment suitable for everyone. Instead it produces two distinct types of job. One set consists of the secure, permanent, high-skilled and well-paid tasks. Another consists largely of the temporary, hard, and unpleasant tasks that few people want to do, and which are also poorly paid. In English the latter jobs are often referred to as the 'three Ds' – dirty, dangerous and difficult. In Japanese they are the 'three K's' – *kitanai, kiden,* and *kitsu*[1]. Unsurprisingly, most locals want to do the permanent well-paid jobs and prefer to steer clear of the 3-Ds and the 3-Ks and their equivalents in other languages. Nevertheless these jobs still need doing and, as a result, rich countries often have shortages of construction workers, or office cleaners, or dishwashers. One solution would be for employers to increase the wages for the worst jobs until sufficient people were tempted to take them. However, if they increase the wages of the people at the bottom of the ladder, they will also have to pay more to the workers higher up so as to maintain their differentials. Employers are happier therefore to keep as clear a distinction as possible between the two sets of jobs – hence the 'dual' labor market.

One way of keeping the jobs separate in the past was to employ women or young people to do the worst and most unstable jobs. Nowadays that is less easy. More women want permanent work, and young people also want to do something better. Moreover, with birth rates falling in many countries, teenagers are becoming scarcer. A neater solution is to use immigrant workers, who are not so choosy about what they are prepared to do, and are less preoccupied with job security or a career path. Hence the people cleaning the offices in Geneva are more likely to be Portuguese or Moroccan than Swiss. And the people picking oranges in the burgeoning orchards around Chiang Mai in northern Thailand are not local Thais, who have lost interest in that kind of low-paid work, but invariably Burmese who have slipped across the border to earn two or three times more than they can at home.

Both the individual and the structural perspectives offer some insight into migration. But it is difficult to keep them distinct. People's choices are certainly shaped by external forces, but different people respond in different ways to the same pressures. In any case, whether acting as individuals or as groups they can also reshape their own destinies. One example of the overlap between the individual and the structural is the development of migrant networks. What often happens is that one adventurous, or desperate, person or family settles arbitrarily in a new place. If these pioneers are successful, they then send the word back to others, triggering a sequence of 'chain migration'. In fact few migrants travel without overseas contacts – people who can help them find accommodation and employment. In this case, individuals making their own choices eventually build up a migration structure all of their own.

If you think this is all too simple, however, there are even grander propositions, like the dauntingly-titled 'world systems theory'. The systems view incorporates not just individual decision-making and migrant networks, but also weaves in flows of capital and goods, and attempts to show how these all fit together and merge with political and cultural factors into one seamless whole. This is most useful when considering the migration flows in a fairly limited area, between North Africa and Europe, say, or between the Polynesian Islands and Aotearoa/New Zealand. But when extended to larger areas such theories become hopelessly complex and any diagram that tries to illustrate the myriad connections starts to look like a map of the London underground merged with a spider's web. Everything in the world is in some way connected to everything else, but accepting this does not get you very far. In these circumstances it is probably easier to consider some of the distinct factors that contribute to migration and then imagine how they fit together in various combinations. The most obvious starting point is the wage gap between rich and poor countries.

Gaps in earnings between rich and poor

Most labor migrants are traveling to earn more money, so you would expect them to move from the poorest countries to the richest ones. The crudest way they could assess the earnings potential in different countries is by comparing per capita Gross Domestic Products (GDPs). The GDP is the sum total of what everyone in the country makes or sells – usually expressed in US dollars – which can then be divided by the number of people to give the average national income. However, this gives a misleading picture since a dollar stretches further in one country than another, so the per capita GDP is commonly adjusted to take account of 'purchasing power parity' (PPP). After this correction, the richest country in the world turns out to be Luxembourg whose per capita GDP in 1998 was $PPP 33,505. The poorest country is less easy to identify since there are a number of candidates, all of whom have per capita GPDs around the $400 mark, but it could be Ethiopia at $PPP 383.

Of course a migrant going to a country does not immediately earn the average national income. He or she will get a better idea of the prospects by looking at actual wages for the kind of job they might do. This information is not collected very systematically or regularly, but table 2.1 overleaf attempts to gather some of this data by listing the average hourly wage costs in manufacturing. Wage costs are not the same as wages since they also include what the employer has to pay in pension and social security contributions, but one way or another a high proportion of these costs will finish up in the worker's pocket[i]. A potential migrant looking at this table might conclude that the best place to work in 1995 was Germany. An employer on the other hand, who was looking for cheap labor, would be more interested in setting up shop in China or India. You can also see how over the period 1980-95 wages rose steeply in Singapore and South Korea, which explains why these have recently been attracting many migrants.

If you migrated to Germany would you really earn that much? Probably not. As the dual labor market theory suggests, immigrants do not get the best jobs since local workers get first pick. And even when immigrants are doing the same jobs as locals, they frequently earn less. In South Korea in 1999, for example, workers from Thailand, China and Pakistan employed officially on public works programs were paid only 45 to 76 per cent of what Korean workers earned. Thus foreign carpenters were paid $636 per

Table 2.1 – Hourly wage costs in manufacturing, 1980-95			
	1980	1985	1995
	$	$	$
Settlement countries			
Aotearoa/N. Zealand	5.3	4.5	10.1
Australia	8.5	8.2	14.4
Canada	8.7	10.9	16.0
United States	9.9	13.0	17.2
Europe			
Austria	8.9	7.6	25.3
Belgium	13.1	9.0	26.9
Denmark	10.8	8.1	24.2
Finland	8.2	8.2	24.8
France	8.9	5.7	19.3
Germany	12.3	9.6	31.9
Italy	8.2	7.6	16.5
Netherlands	12.1	8.8	24.2
Norway	11.6	10.4	24.4
Spain	5.9	4.7	12.7
Sweden	12.5	9.7	21.4
Switzerland	11.1	9.7	29.3
United Kingdom	7.6	6.3	13.8
Czech Republic	..	..	1.3
Hungary	..	..	1.7
Poland	..	..	2.1
Russia	..	..	0.6

month, compared with \$1,500 for Korean carpenters[2]. The chances of being exploited are even greater if you are in the country illegally. In Hong Kong in 2000 while the normal rate for day laboring was \$28, mainland Chinese working in a wholesale market were earning only \$8 a day for unloading vegetables from trucks[3].

Nevertheless, immigrants, even unskilled ones, will often earn far more than they did at home. One of the largest wage gaps between two neighboring countries is between the US and Mexico: an average factory worker in the US earns around four times as much as a Mexican factory worker – and 30 times more than a Mexican agricultural worker[4]. Within Europe, one of the most significant wage gaps is across the Germany-

	1980	1985	1995
	$	$	$
Asia			
China	0.3	0.2	0.3
Hong Kong	1.5	1.7	4.8
India	0.4	0.4	0.3
Indonesia	0.2	0.2	0.3
Japan	5.5	6.3	23.7
Korea, South	1.0	1.2	7.4
Malaysia	0.7	1.1	1.6
Philippines	0.5	0.6	0.7
Singapore	1.5	2.5	7.3
Taiwan	1.0	1.5	5.8
Thailand	0.3	0.5	0.5
Latin America			
Argentina	0.5	0.7	1.7
Brazil	1.7	1.3	4.3
Chile	1.8	1.9	3.6
Colombia	0.1	0.3	0.5
Mexico	2.2	1.6	1.5
Peru	0.6	0.3	1.2
Venezuela	3.7	2.3	1.7

Note: ·· = not available

Morgan Stanley and Co. Inc., 1996.

Poland border: Polish factory workers earn around $250 per month, but if they spend their holidays in Germany picking asparagus they can get $800 to $900 a month[5]. Similarly, unskilled workers in Malaysia earn around $100 a month at home but $600 a month in Singapore[6].

These gaps are large and tempting. Does this mean that migration will continue until wages everywhere have been equalized? Historically this has not been the case. In Europe during the 1960s and 1970s, millions of workers went from Spain and Italy to France and West Germany. But as incomes rose in the poorer countries, fewer people chose to leave, even though significant wage gaps remained. Workers do not only think about their immediate income, they are also looking to the future. When the home country starts to do better and local prospects brighten, people become more optimistic and prefer to stay at home.

More jobs than workers

Prospective migrants do not of course only look at the gap in wages, they also have to consider the prospect of actually finding work. Are there any vacancies? To some extent this is a question of economic cycles. When an economy starts to expand, employment opportunities increase and eventually there are more jobs than workers. The post-war boom in Europe, for example, soon created far more jobs than could be filled by local people. France and West Germany suddenly found they needed many more workers than even Spain or Italy could provide, and started recruiting 'guest workers' from North Africa, Turkey and elsewhere. This economic expansion lasted until 1973, when the sudden hike in the price of oil reduced the need for extra labor. By that time West Germany and France had around 2.5 million foreign workers accounting for 10-12 per cent of their labor forces.

During the same period, the United Kingdom also

went out of its way to attract people. In the 1950s London Transport, for example, actively recruited staff in the West Indies. And in the 1960s the garment factories in the north and the midlands of England drew in hundreds of thousands of people from the Indian subcontinent. By 1962, when the first round of immigration controls were introduced, the United Kingdom had absorbed around half a million immigrants from the 'New Commonwealth'.

After 1973 with the rise in the price of oil, the demand for workers slackened throughout Europe, but then correspondingly took off in the countries of the Gulf. Flush with their new wealth, the oil-exporters suddenly needed millions of workers of all kinds particularly to build the new houses, offices and hotels. At first the Gulf countries drew in workers from other Arab states, but when they had exhausted these possibilities they then looked to the Indian subcontinent and other countries in Asia. When the price of oil fell in the 1980s, the Gulf countries needed fewer construction workers but by that point local people had grown accustomed to a higher standard of living and were making much more use of hotels and restaurants. They also found it difficult to manage without the convenience of maids and chauffeurs. As a result, by 1985 the largest proportion of immigrant workers in the Gulf were employed in services.

By the late 1980s, the focus of intense economic development had moved on, this time to Southeast Asia itself. The 'tiger' economies of Singapore, Taiwan, South Korea, and Hong Kong were roaring ahead and they too soon found themselves short of workers. The clearest example of this is South Korea. During the 1960s and 1970s South Korea sent millions of its own workers overseas to the Middle East and elsewhere. But from the mid-1980s Koreans found there were far more jobs at home and they had less cause to leave (figure 2.1 overleaf)[7]. By the early 1990s Korea itself faced severe labor shortages particularly in

Koreans stay at home

In its earlier years of industrialization South Korea sent millions of migrants to other countries, mainly to the Gulf for construction work. But during the 1980s, as Korea became richer, people preferred to stay at home. Nowadays Korea itself attracts immigrants from many other Asian countries, particularly China. ■

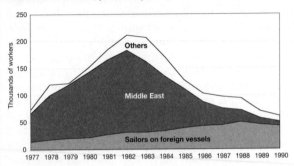

Figure 2.1 – Emigration from South Korea, 1977-90

Park (1991)

the garment factories, in coal mining and in construction. At first the Korean government resisted employing foreigners, but this just meant that employers had to use undocumented workers, most of whom arrived on 14-day tourist visas from China, the Philippines and elsewhere, and extended their 'holidays'. The most obvious source of workers for Korea is China since there are around two million ethnic Koreans in China; for them, the choice between $2 per day planting rice in Chinese fields and $50 per day on a Korean construction site is not a difficult decision.

Even during an economic boom, however, the 'dual labor market' persists. Most immigrants find they have to do the worst jobs – the 3-D tasks. Native (local) workers shun such jobs partly because they are inherently unpleasant, and low-paid. But also because succeeding generations have higher aspirations. As their education levels rise, so young people reject the work that their parents did – indeed parents demand that their offspring look for something better.

The 3-D work can also be very unstable. This is most evident in construction. Property developers typically finance their activities with borrowed money, so when there is an economic downturn, or a financial crisis that pushes up interest rates, many speculative building projects suddenly become unviable. When the Asian financial bubble burst in 1997 the most visible evidence of the crisis was along the skylines of Bangkok and Seoul where immobile cranes hovered silently over half-completed skyscrapers.

Agriculture is another 3-D job, but is more stable. Farmers have mechanized as much as they can but still need migrant workers, particularly for picking crops. California, for example, grows around one-quarter of the world's commercial strawberries, a crop that is too soft for machine harvesting and needs around 2,000 worker-hours per acre. This is provided almost entirely by Mexican immigrants who are paid around $200 per week. A survey by the US Department of Labor in the early 1990s concluded that of the 670,000 migrant farm workers in the United States, around 85 per cent were immigrants – and more than half of these were undocumented[8]. Many other countries rely on immigrant labor for agriculture. Around 80 per cent of the coffee in the Dominican Republic, for example, is picked by Haitians[9]. And Chinese workers from Manchuria are to be found planting water melons across the border in Russia.

European farms also depend on immigrants. In the south of Spain, for example, farmers growing fruit and vegetables in plastic greenhouses are mostly hiring Moroccan day laborers. British farmers make less use of immigrant labor. Officially only 10,000 temporary immigrant farm workers were allowed into the UK in 2000, though the number will rise to 15,200 in 2001. But the National Farmers Union has been lobbying the government to allow in more foreign farm workers because at the height of the season there are not enough people to pick all the fruit and vegetables.

Meanwhile, British farmers have to rely on illegal immigrants from Eastern Europe who enter the country as tourists after being recruited by 'gangmasters'.

After construction and agriculture, probably the next largest employer of immigrant labor is in various forms of personal services – from nurses, to gardeners, to nannies to maids. These one-to-one service jobs are even more difficult to mechanize and the demand seems to be rising steadily. Near the top of the hierarchy are the health services which in most countries have a disproportionately high share of immigrant staff – represented in the US TV hospital drama *ER* by a dashing Croatian doctor. The British National Health Service (NHS) has always been underpinned by immigrant staff: 31 per cent of doctors and 13 per cent of nurses are foreign-born, and in London the proportions are even higher – 23 and 47 per cent respectively. Over the past decade, of the 16,000 new staff recruited by the NHS, half qualified abroad[10].

In some cases medical staff are happy to move around to gain greater experience but the salary differentials also help. In the early 1990s a staff nurse in Manila would get only $146 per month at home, while she or he could earn around $500 in the Gulf, and $3,000 in the United States. Unsurprisingly, the Philippines in recent decades has been exporting nurses at a rapid rate – 3,000 or more per year. Given the ageing populations in most of the developed countries, the need for nurses can only increase.

With many more women taking full-time jobs there is also a growing demand for nannies. This was highlighted in the United States in 1993 when the Attorney-General was found to have employed an illegal immigrant as a nanny. At present many child-care workers – around 8,000 a year – enter the US as au pairs. This is in theory an educational exchange with a 'child-care component' since the au pair is supposed to be treated like a member of the family. But this does not always work out well – as shown in 1997 by the case of Louise Woodward, a British au pair who killed the child under her care and was eventually convicted of manslaughter. Nannies are also finding work in many other countries. Jamaican women have been attracted to Canada as nannies, not least because once they have worked there for two years under contract they are eligible to apply for immigrant status.

Further down the employment ladder are foreign maids. Families in many countries have grown accustomed to the convenience of a domestic servant, and when local people are no longer prepared to serve, foreigners provide a good substitute. Since the maids work closely with their clients, a degree of compatibility helps. Filipinos who speak English are very popular in a number of countries: in Malaysia, for example, Filipino maids earn around 60 per cent more than Indonesian maids. If Malaysians are Muslims they are obliged to employ a Muslim maid, though they are also allowed to employ Filipinos or Sri Lankans for other tasks – to cook certain dishes, perhaps, or to wash the dog.

Hong Kong also has around 200,000 foreign maids, and though the majority are Filipinos these are gradually being replaced by mainland Chinese[11]. The disadvantage for maids living in close proximity to their clients is that they are frequently subjected to physical and sexual abuse, as well as just being treated unfairly: the *South China Morning Post* reported in June 2000 that nine out of 10 Indonesian maids in Hong Kong were underpaid, with many receiving half the legal minimum wage[12].

Another well-established job for immigrants is as cleaners, or 'janitors'. In the United States, most of these are now employed by 'building maintenance contractors'. This is an industry rife with complex forms of subcontracting, often designed to avoid paying social security contributions. Some cleaning companies pay subcontractors only $7 an hour per worker. In turn the subcontractors might pay the workers $5 per hour[13]. In the United States a high proportion of janitors come from Mexico, and are undocumented immigrants. But the situation is similar elsewhere: in Italy around one-third of cleaners are immigrants.

Construction work, agriculture, and cleaning services are typical immigrant tasks in most countries. But other professions can gradually become 'immigrant jobs'. Until the mid-1980s, taxi driving, for example, was a well-respected blue-collar job in the United States and attracted whites and blacks alike. But over the last 25 years the Taxi Operators Association estimates that the proportion of drivers in Washington, DC, who are foreign-born has risen from 25 per cent to 85 per cent . In New York, more than 90 per cent of the 45,000 taxi drivers are now foreign-born[14].

Employers have to recruit immigrants when local people refuse to do the work but they are also

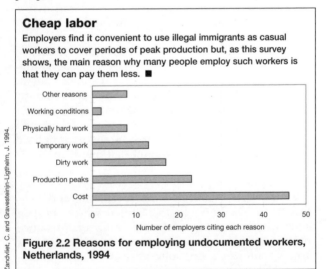

Cheap labor

Employers find it convenient to use illegal immigrants as casual workers to cover periods of peak production but, as this survey shows, the main reason why many people employ such workers is that they can pay them less. ∎

Zandvliet, C. and Gravesteinjn-Ligthelm, J. 1994.

Figure 2.2 Reasons for employing undocumented workers, Netherlands, 1994

attracted by the low cost. A survey in the Netherlands asked 84 employers why they took on undocumented immigrants (figure 2.2). Their main reason was that legal employees were too expensive, especially for the catering and garment industries, but they also liked the flexibility of hiring people to work in unpleasant jobs for short periods to help them cover production peaks[15].

Shaking people loose

The attraction of higher wages, and the demand for workers in richer countries are probably the main driving forces behind international migration. But for people to move they must be mobile. Often they have little choice. They might, for example, lose their land because they have fallen into debt. Or if their parents fall sick and die, children will suddenly be forced to fend for themselves. But beyond personal catastrophes there are also broader forces at work – shaking up settled communities and opening up new horizons.

In many ways the situation for developing countries is similar to that of 19th-century Europe following the industrial revolution, when people who could no longer find work in the countryside flocked to smoky factories in the cities. Not everyone could find work there, so many looked overseas. Over the period 1846-90 around 17 million people left Europe for North America. Half came from the British Isles, partly because Britain was the first country to industrialize, but also because of the Irish potato famine of 1845-47. Table 2.2 overleaf traces this process, taking as a marker for the onset of the industrial revolution in each country the year when railway tracks first exceeded 620 miles (1,000 kilometers). This shows the wave of industrialization passing across Europe, to be followed by mass emigration. The average time lag between the onset of industrialization and the year of peak emigration was 28 years[16].

Table 2.2 – Emigration and the industrial revolution

	Year when railway tracks exceeded 620 miles (1,000 km)	Year when emigrants first exceeded 1,000 people	Year of peak emigration
British Isles	1838	1827	1851
Germany	1843	1834	1854
France	1846	1846	1851
Austria-Hungary	1847	1880	1907
Russia-Poland	1851	1882	1913
Italy	1854	1880	1907
Spain	1859	1917	1921
Switzerland	1860	1881	1883
Netherlands	1870	1882	1882
Denmark	1874	1882	1882
Portugal	1878	1912	1921

Massey (1988)

The same processes are at work in developing countries today, and are even more rapid. Every year around 30 million people in developing countries migrate to towns and cities. The proportion of people living in urban areas has been growing rapidly: in 1960 it was 22 per cent; by 1994 it was 37 per cent; and by 2025 it is expected to reach about 60 per cent[17]. Most of today's 'megalopolises' are in developing countries and they are expanding with explosive speed. London, for example, which was the first city in the world to pass the one-million mark, took 130 years to reach a population of 8 million. Mexico City, on the other hand grew from 1 million to 15 million in just 50 years[18].

Heading for the city is usually a good idea. Not only can migrants earn more, they also stand a better chance of receiving health care and education for their children. Even so most will find only low-paid, casual employment in the 'informal sector', as day laborers, or street vendors, or rickshaw-pullers. The International Labour Organization estimates that at the end of 1998 up to 900 million people around the world were 'underemployed' – which means that they were working substantially less than full time and wanted to work longer, or were earning less than a living wage[19]. For those who have reached the city, and not found satisfactory work, the next logical step is to travel even further afield. They might not be able to do this straight away, since they will be unable to afford the traveling expenses. But when they have been uprooted once, and seen what is on offer elsewhere, and have developed the necessary skills and contacts, their options become much wider.

Developing countries today face an altogether more complex situation, primarily because their process of modernization has largely been shaped by technologies and ideas imported from – or imposed by – the industrial countries. Added to this there have been profound demographic changes, largely as a result of falling death rates, that have triggered rapid increases in population size. Nevertheless, the underlying principle is similar: economic and social development disrupts settled societies and creates the conditions for mass migration.

This disruption has been magnified in recent years by the impact of globalization and liberalization, particularly on agriculture. Most agriculture in Mexico, for example, consists of the production of corn and beans on small plots that have not operated very efficiently by market criteria. During the 1970s the farmers working on communally-owned plots, the *ejidos*, could bank on a lot of support from the government which subsidized inputs such as seeds and fertilizers and then bought the crop at a guaranteed price, before selling it at a lower price to urban consumers. But when Mexico became ensnared in the debt crisis in the 1980s the government had to cut subsidies for electricity, fertilizers and seeds. Faced with rising costs, the farmers with the least-fertile land soon found they were losing money. When Mexico joined the North American Free Trade Agreement (NAFTA) in 1994, the reforms were even more disruptive. Now small Mexican farmers found themselves competing with the highly mechanized prairie farmers in the United States and Canada. Ironically, in the United States such farmers were far more heavily subsidized – in 1995 by around $30,000 per farm[20].

Mexican farmers had already been leaving agriculture for the cities, and were more free to do so because the government had also removed restrictions on land ownership so that individual farmers could sell or rent out the former *ejido* land. Now the exodus became a flood. By 1996, around 750,000 subsistence farmers had already left agriculture – and many of these headed for the United States, where they found themselves working as agricultural laborers[21]. The liberalization of the international trade in food has similarly ominous implications for small farmers all over the world. In 2001, international food prices were the lowest that they had been for decades; good news for food consumers, but bad news for farmers trying to maintain sustainable systems of agriculture.

Another aspect of modernization that encourages and sustains migration is the proliferation of global media and the revolutions in telecommunications and transport. Anyone who watches TV or goes to the cinema in a developing country could get the impression that the industrial countries offer easy, unlimited wealth. Some parts of North Africa, for example, can pick up Spanish television. As one Spanish Civil Guard commander commented, 'they see that and they think it is paradise'[22].

Some governments have also used TV to dissuade immigration. The US Immigration Service places ads on Mexican television in the border areas warning of the dangers of crossing the desert. And Australia in 2000 ran a similar campaign in the Middle East and Central Asia, warning about the hazards of arriving illegally by boat – as well as the risk of being greeted in Australia by poisonous snakes, spiders and crocodiles. In practice, most emigrants probably have a fairly realistic idea of what to expect when they arrive.

Nevertheless such images, positive and negative, add to a more worldly outlook – a sense that foreign countries are no longer entirely alien places.

A combination of disparities between rich and poor countries, and the upheavals of modernization and globalization, are therefore creating the conditions for emigration from the poorer countries. But which countries do they migrate from, and where do they go and why? That is the subject of the next chapter.

1 Morgan Stanley, 1996. 'The great global restructuring debate', in *US Investment Research*, New York, 11 October. **2** *Migration News* (1999). Vol. 6, No. 2, February. **3** Lo, C. (2000). 'Illegal workers paid three times less at local markets', in *South China Morning Post*, March 22. **4** Borjas, G. (2000). 'Mexico's one-way remedy', in *New York Times*, July 18. **5** *Migration News* (2000). Vol. 7, No. 6, June. **6** *Migration News* (2000). Vol. 7, No. 8, August. **7** Park, Y. (1991). *Foreign Labor in Korea: Issues and Policy Options*, paper presented to the Second Japan-ASEAN Forum on International Labor Migration in East-Asia, Tokyo. UNU/ILO **8** Gabbard, Susan, Mines, R. and Boccalandro B. (1994). *Migrant Farmworkers: Pursuing Security in an Unstable Labor Market*. ASP Research Report 5, Washington DC. US Department of Labor. **9** *Migration News* (2000). Vol. 4, No. 4, April. **10** Glover, S., C. Gott, A. Loizillon, Portes, R. Price, S. Spencer, V. Srinivasan and C. Willis (2001). *Migration: An Economic and Social Analysis*. RDS Occasional Paper No 67. London, Home Office. **11** Castles, Stephen (1998). *New Migrations, Ethnicity and Nationalism in Southeast and East Asia*, paper based on a talk given to the Transnational Communities Programme, School of Geography, Oxford University. **12** Kwok, Yenni (2000) 'On hire to the cruellest bidder,' *South China Morning Post*, June 7. **13** Cleeland, N. (2000), 'Heartache on Aisle 3: Sweatshop for Janitors,' *Los Angeles Times*, July 2. **14** Glass, S. (1996). 'Taxis and the meaning of work,' in *The New Republic* p. 21. **15** Zandvliet, C. and Gravesteinjn-Ligthelm, J. (1994). *Illegal Employment in the Netherlands: Extent and Effects*, A study commissioned by the Ministry of Social Affairs & Employment and the Ministry of Justice, The Hague. **16** Massey, D. (1988). 'Economic development and international migration in comparative perspective', in *Population and Development Review*, Vol. 14, No. 2, New York. **17** United Nations, (1994). *World Urbanization Prospects: The 1994 Revision*, United Nations Population Division, New York. **18** Camp, S. (1990). *Cities: Life in the World's Largest Metropolitan Areas*, Population Action International, Washington, DC. **19** ILO (2000). *World Labour Report*, Geneva. **20** Oxfam, (1996). *Trade Liberalization as a Threat to Livelihoods: The Corn Sector in the Philippines*, Oxford, Oxfam **21** *Migration News* (1996). Vol. 3, No. 10. October. **22** Stalker, P. (1994). *The Work of Strangers*, Geneva, ILO.

3 Choosing the destination

Migrants have a world to choose from, but they tend to follow well-established routes – based on historical ties and on the networks created by earlier pioneers. And although they can travel independently, many now enlist the help of labor brokers, or smugglers, or fall into the hands of traffickers.

INTERNATIONAL MIGRANTS HAVE predictable destinations. Malians tend to go to Côte d'Ivoire; Colombians to Venezuela; Tongans to Aotearoa/New Zealand; Turks to Germany. Some simply go to the nearest country – and if the distances are short enough they may even commute. People from Malmo in Sweden, for example, travel daily to jobs in Copenhagen where they can earn higher wages. Meanwhile, French, Belgian and German *frontaliers* (border commuters) are traveling daily into Luxembourg where they make up one-quarter of the labor force. In these cases passport checks are cursory or non-existent. But international migration is even more casual when the travelers are unaware that they are crossing national borders. Nomadic herders in the Sahel region of West Africa drift back and forth between Niger, Mali and Chad, seeking pasture and water for their animals, paying scant regard to frontiers. Most borders in Africa are very porous and members of extended families are often to be found on either side.

In some cases the journeys may actually be more persistent than the borders. Thus the mainland Chinese who come into Hong Kong every day have ceased to be international migrants now that Hong Kong is part of China. On the other hand the chances of crossing international frontiers have multiplied with the increasing number of nation states. In 1945 the United Nations had just 45 members but by 2000 the number had swollen to 189 and is likely to increase further. Should Palestine finally gain its independence, for example, the thousands of Palestinians who work – or at least want to work – in Israel will become international commuters.

Following colonial paths

The migrant's choice of destination can also be influenced by historical – and particularly colonial – links. Many African migrants head for France, for example, treading paths that France itself established decades ago. During the First World War, France had drafted so many of its own citizens into the army that it ran short of workers in agriculture, industry and construction, so had to bring in Africans from its colonies to take their place. When the war was over, Africans, having spotted an interesting alternative to plantation work, continued to head for France. The United Kingdom has also recruited from its former colonies. During the Second World War the UK not only made use of colonial subjects as soldiers, it also recruited men from the Caribbean to work in munitions factories and in Scottish forests. After the war the UK continued to recruit from the West Indies to meet labor shortages in transport and in the National Health Service.

The United States had fewer colonies but has nevertheless held sway over many countries, particularly Mexico. At the beginning of the last century, when US farmers and railroad owners were running short of labor, they sent recruiting teams south of the border to find workers. Later, in the 1940s, the US organized the more formal *Bracero* program to bring in Mexicans to work as seasonal laborers. For a long time any Mexican who crossed the Santa Fe bridge between Juarez and El Paso was not detained by the Immigration and Naturalization Service but enthusiastically offered work. Germany also has a limited colonial history and has had to send recruiters to other countries to find workers, most notably in the 1960s and early 1970s when it wooed workers from

Turkey to come temporarily as *gastarbeiters* (guestwork-ers). In all these cases, the labor-receiving countries took the initiative. Indeed the industrialized countries deliberately started almost all the major international flows of migrants of the past century[1]. Once they had established the routes and the links, however, the migration flows took on a life of their own.

Bringing families together

One factor that tends to reinforce historical patterns is that the migrant-receiving countries give priority to reuniting families. This arises at least in part from a greater respect for human rights. Article 13 of the Universal Declaration of Human Rights establishes that everyone has the right to leave any country. It does not offer the corresponding right to enter anoth-er country other than as a refugee. But Article 16 says that everyone has the right to marry and that the fam-ily is the 'fundamental group unit of society' entitled to protection from the state. The European Convention for the Protection of Human Rights also establishes that everyone has the right to be with their own families, and Article 19 of the European Social Charter says that countries must make every effort to help migrant workers legally settled in a country to be reunited with their families. Similarly, the ILO Migrant Workers Recommendation of 1975 urges countries to facilitate family reunification.

Beyond any desire to fulfill human rights there are also sound social reasons for allowing migrants to be with their families, since workers with families tend to lead more stable lives and are better integrated with the communities in which they live. As a result, the eas-iest way to be accepted legally as an immigrant to any country is to be closely related either to a citizen of that country, or to an immigrant who already has rights of residence.

This has had a profound influence on modern pat-terns of migration. In 1998, family entry accounted for two-thirds of all immigration into the United States, and for over one-quarter of all immigration into Australia and Canada. This is demonstrated in table 3.1, which shows the main categories of immigration to the US in the 1990s. There are two main types of family entry. First, US citizens are entitled to bring in 'immediate relatives', which includes their spouses and unmarried minor children, and there are no limits to the number of people who can come in each year under this category. Second, US citizens can also bring in other relatives, including adult offspring, though these have a weaker claim and only a certain number are admitted each year.

Table 3.1 – Inflows of permanent settlers to the United States 1990-98 ('000s)

	1990	1991	1992	1993	1994	1995	1996	1997	1998
Immediate relatives of US citizens[a]	232	237	236	255	250	220	300	322	284
Relative preferences[b]	215	216	213	227	212	238	294	213	192
Total family	446	453	449	482	462	459	595	536	476
Workers' preference	58	60	116	147	123	85	118	91	78
Refugees	97	139	117	127	121	115	129	112	55
Legalization[c]	880	1,123	163	24	6	4	5	3	1
Others	54	52	129	124	92	58	71	57	52
TOTAL	1,537	1,827	974	904	804	721	916	798	661

Notes:
(a) Numerically unrestricted immigrants, comprising spouses, unmarried minor children, and orphans adopted by US citizens as well as parents of adult US citizens.
(b) Numerically restricted relatives comprise the following four preference classes: i) Unmarried adult sons and daughters of US citizens; ii) Spouses and unmarried sons and daughters of permanent resident aliens; iii) Married sons and daughters of US citizens; iv) Brothers and sisters of adult US citizens.
(c) Under the 1986 Immigration Reform and Control Act, foreigners who had been accorded temporary legal status could apply, between December 1988 and December 1990, for a permanent residence permit.

SOPEMI (2000)

Although all countries accept the principle of family reunification, some are more liberal than others. The German and French governments have been more restrictive, and in the 1970s both tried to cut back rights to family reunification until these attempts were struck down by the courts on legal and constitutional grounds. France still has a fairly restrictive policy that does not even allow automatic entry for parents or brothers and sisters. Australia and the Netherlands, on the other hand, extend rights of reunification to gay partners. In the United Kingdom, people who are already settled have a right to bring in their dependant children and spouses and, under certain circumstances, their parents, grandparents and other relatives. In 1999, about 65,000 family members were allowed to enter the UK – 25,000 were wives, 15,000 were husbands, 20,000 were children and 4,000 were parents, grandparents and other dependants[2].

You might expect that the emphasis on family reunion would reproduce and intensify the historical links between sending and receiving countries, and freeze the immigration pattern. But not necessarily. Some nationalities are more family-minded than others. The United States discovered this after 1965 when it fundamentally changed the basis of immigration policy. Until that point, the United States based the share of visas for people coming from outside the Americas on the proportion that each nationality had achieved in the US population by 1920. This meant that it gave more than 70 per cent of visas to three countries – the United Kingdom, Ireland and Germany – while offering 1 per cent to Africa and 2 per cent to the whole of Asia. By the 1960s there was increasing opposition to this fundamentally racist policy and in 1965 the US passed the Immigration and Nationality Act. Henceforth immigration would be based not on national origin, race or ancestry, but on allocations for certain categories of workers, combined with the kind of family preference system indicated in table 3.1.

At this point, the US government assumed that family preference would continue to tilt the balance in favor of Europe. Senator Robert Kennedy, for example, estimated that in the first year perhaps 5,000 people would come from Asia and the Pacific, 'but we do not expect that there would be a great influx after that'. In fact, Asians rapidly started to dominate the flows. A million or more had arrived as refugees from Vietnam, Cambodia and Laos, and they, along with the existing Filipino and Korean communities, were very keen to sponsor the arrival of other family members. Asians brought in four times as many relatives per primary immigrant as Europeans and Latin Americans[3].

Migrant networks

Migrants' choices of destination are also powerfully influenced by migrant networks. People are most likely to go to places where they will be welcomed and helped by friends, relatives and compatriots – capitalizing on niche communities and transnational links that have been established by early pioneers. Nowadays, relatively few people travel without a contact in their destination country.

One study of Filipino migrants to the United States, for example, concluded that when people wanted to know the details of regulations and visas they would by-pass the US embassy or the travel agents and instead rely on the practical experience of Filipinos who had themselves been through the process[4]. Similar conclusions have been found from many other places. Figure 3.1 overleaf shows the result of recent research among migrants from Turkey, Morocco, Egypt, Ghana and Senegal who had moved to Spain and Italy. This study confirms that the primary sources of information are family members in the destination country[5]. It also found that the migrants did not actually know much about official immigration regulations. Nowadays immigration to Europe is so restricted that it is scarcely worth knowing what the

Travel advice

The most practical information on destination countries, and how to get there, comes from family members and other travelers. A survey of migrants from Turkey, Morocco, Egypt, Ghana and Senegal to Spain and Italy found that more than two-thirds had gained information principally from family members, whether in the home or the destination country. ■

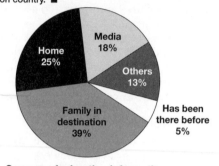

Figure 3.1 – Sources of migration information

rules are; more useful is to know how to bypass them.

The networks are of great importance for helping immigrants settle in their new communities, and one of the first things that the compatriots will do is to find accommodation. A 1990 study of Brazilian immigrants to Canada, for example, found that 30 per cent stayed with friends when they first arrived, while another 20 per cent were put up by relatives[6]. But probably the most important thing the networks do is to help the immigrants find work, often with the previous generation of immigrants. In Los Angeles, for example around one-third of employed Koreans in the early 1990s found jobs with fellow Koreans[7]. This works out well not just for the workers but also for the immigrant entrepreneurs, who believe that they are getting trustworthy compatriots as staff.

But immigrant networks also act as efficient employment exchanges for many other enterprises. Mexicans in the US are very adroit at this. Immigrant workers often know which of their friends is considering moving on, and can line up a replacement. The *New York Times* quoted a supervisor in a printing plant: 'The referrals occur before the vacancy appears. Everybody out there knows it before we do'[8]. One advantage of this system for the employer is that the network puts peer-group pressure on the new arrivals; if they don't perform well they will fall out of favor with the compatriots who found them the job.

Immigrants recruited in this way tend to group themselves in clusters. A meat-packing plant at Storm Lake, Iowa, for example, by the early 1990s finished up with a workforce that was one-quarter Lao refugees. In this case an early settler from Laos in Storm Lake achieved an influential position and drew many other Lao into the factory. Around 125 of the 149 Lao heads of households in the area worked at the plant[9]. Immigrant groups will come together even when they start out separated. This is a familiar phenomenon with refugee groups who may initially have been dispersed, but tend subsequently to regroup in the largest cities where they can find ethnic enterprises and community associations[10].

Networks not only cluster immigrants geographically, they also slot them into particular employment niches. By the mid-1990s almost half of the economy motels in the US were owned by Indians, a high proportion of the fruit and vegetable shops in many cities were owned by Koreans, and if you went into a doughnut shop in California you were very likely to be served by a Cambodian. But the same phenomenon appears in most other countries that absorb large numbers of immigrants. The classification in box 2.1 overleaf was the assessment of South Africa's *Weekly Mail and Guardian* of the nationalities of immigrants in various professions[11].

Sent by the state

In addition to the informal recruitment networks, there are also more formal state-organized systems.

Box 2.1

Immigrant niches in South Africa

The *Weekly Mail and Guardian* in South Africa identifies the following migrant specialties:

Laborers

Mines: Basotho (Lesotho), Mozambicans and Swazis

Farms: Men, women and children from Mozambique and Zimbabwe

Gardeners: Malawians and Zimbabweans who work mostly in Johannesburg's suburbs.

Domestic workers: Malawians; Swazis

Entrepreneurs and artisans

Craft: Zimbabweans, Malawians, Swazis

Grey goods: (including hi-fis, TVs, computers and cell phones): Indians, Pakistanis, Hausas

Cigarettes, sweets: Somalis

Knock-offs (cheap imitations of labeled goods): Taiwanese

Shadow economy

Cocaine/other drugs: Nigerians; Moroccans

Sharkfin/perlemoen poaching: Taiwanese

Satellite, cell phone and land-line tele-shops (usually run from houses): Nigerians, Indians, Pakistanis

Passport rackets: Congolese

Prostitution: Mozambican women from Nampula province in the north, Zimbabwean women and eastern Europeans.

Governments of a number of sending countries, particularly in Asia, have gone out of their way to promote labor exports. Until the 1980s, South Korea's Overseas Development Corporation, for example, would act on behalf of foreign employers by recruiting Korean workers. In addition Korean construction companies would also send laborers to work on overseas projects. Nowadays the bulk of such state-sponsored workers come from Vietnam and China. The Vietnamese government used to send many workers to Eastern Europe, but following the collapse of communism in Europe the opportunities there dried up and it is having to look for other markets. In 2001, Vietnam was expecting to send around 50,000 workers overseas. Frequently the Vietnamese migrants themselves do not earn very much from this.

If they are being supplied by a Vietnamese company they are only paid at Vietnamese rates, leaving the enterprise to pocket the difference. Either that or they have to pay a large agent's fee to go abroad. China too has organized emigration through state-owned corporations and usually has hundreds of thousands of migrant workers abroad, mostly on labor service agreements or employed by Chinese corporations that have overseas construction contracts.

Governments in a number of other sending countries have also taken a strong interest in labor exports but have exercised control indirectly by regulating private-sector brokers. One of the most active is the Philippine Overseas Employment Administration which licenses and supervises private companies, requiring that they have a minimum amount of capital and that they follow a complex set of regulations. The agency also tries to keep track of the overall flows of migrants and to channel their remittances through the official banking system. It has 33 offices in Asia, the Middle East and Europe to assist Filipino migrants. Other Asian governments, particularly those in South Asia that depend a lot on remittances, also try to promote overseas employment but exercise less control.

Brokered by a body shop

As migration has become more formalized, it has developed into something of an international industry. On the legal side of this business there are now numerous labor brokers prepared to find jobs for workers, or workers for jobs. They operate in sending and the receiving countries – and make their money at both ends. The most conspicuous sign of broker activity in the sending countries is when workers are assembled at the airport. In Dhaka airport in Bangladesh, for example, the men heading for construction sites in Malaysia or Saudi Arabia are hard to miss. They are often neatly kitted out in lurid green tracksuits or spotless tee-shirts emblazoned with the logo of a recruitment agency –

less as an advertising gimmick than to make it easier for the company to identify their charges and shepherd them safely on their way. The Hatta-Soekarno airport in Jakarta offers a similar sight – diminutive, head-scarved Indonesian maids headed for the Gulf can be seen in groups of 20 or 30 hovering around the departure gates.

For an individual looking for a job overseas who has no contacts in the destination country it can make sense to approach a broker, not just to sort out a job but also to arrange transport and accommodation and deal with all the bureaucracy of passports, visas and work permits. This can become very expensive. Migrants sometimes have to pay the equivalent of three or four months' salary up front to the broker – money that they usually have to find by borrowing from other members of their family, or by mortgaging the family house or land. In the Philippines, brokers are allowed by law to charge only the equivalent of a couple of hundred dollars, but Filipino workers in Taiwan in 2001 say they have paid up to $5,000, which is equivalent to around eight months' wages[12]. Once they are in Taiwan, the counterpart of the broker is supposed to continue to help the workers – paying for medical exams, plane tickets home, and also resolving conflicts with employers. But in practice many migrants never even discover who the Taiwanese broker is. In Indonesia in early 2001, for example, the Ministry of Manpower and Transmigration said it would be fining more than 200 labor brokers who had misled or ignored the workers they had sent abroad. In Bangladesh, unskilled workers can pay up $2,000 for a job in Saudi Arabia, which is more than 80 per cent of what they can expect to earn in the first year[13]. Some consider this a price worth paying, but they can also find that they have been deceived and that the work and the conditions are very different from those promised.

Brokers can also be fairly ruthless if the migrant is

unable to repay them from his or her earnings. In April 2001, for example, an Indonesian maid who had been sent to Malaysia was fired by her employer after a month. When she returned to Jakarta she was taken hostage by the broker who demanded $450 for her release. Her mother managed to scrape together $150 but this offer was turned down. The woman was only released after intervention by the Legal Aid Institute for Indonesian Migrant Workers. Even so, the same company was still thought to be holding ten other workers hostage[14].

Some receiving countries have attempted to eliminate the use of brokers. Taiwan, for example, has been trying to clamp down on their activities by negotiating agreements with the governments of Vietnam and the Philippines and encouraging Taiwanese employers to recruit people directly. But workers will probably continue to pay: many start in their own villages by paying the brokers' local contacts just to get a foot on the emigration ladder.

Brokers do not confine their activities to unskilled workers. One of the most lucrative brokering activities at present is to ship Indian computer programmers to the United States. Such workers enter with the 'H-1B' visas for people who have skills that companies are unable to find in the United States. In this case the brokers, called 'body shops', will do most of the work for the company, recruiting the workers and completing the visa formalities. But the programmers effectively remain employees of the brokers. Indian programmers might be grateful for the $50,000 per year they get paid, but they would be even more grateful if they got the $100,000 or more per year that the brokers charge the companies for supplying the workers. In some cases body shops will complete fraudulent H-1B visa applications for fictitious jobs – either in 'paper companies' or in the name of real companies – so as to collect fees from people keen to enter the country, and then hawk their stable of programmers around potential employers[15].

Smugglers, coyotes and snakeheads

Though most brokers get their clients into the destination country legally, others are skilled at smuggling them. Smugglers might hide people in trucks for example, or supply false documents, or bribe immigration officials. At this point it is important to make a distinction between smugglers and traffickers. Smugglers are essentially providing services to willing customers – acting as extra-legal travel agents who offer to transport migrants or asylum-seekers to their chosen destination. Trafficking is a nastier activity – using violence, coercion or deception to buy and sell workers, treating human beings as commodities.

Smugglers are engaged in a dangerous, but usually very profitable, business. Along the 2,000-mile border between Mexico and the United States, they are known as 'coyotes' and offer their clients a selection of entry methods, including floating across the Rio Grande on tire inner tubes, crawling through drainage pipes, or trekking across the desert. They charge a negotiable fee depending on how far the migrant needs escorting – typically $150 to get across the border, $450 to get to San Antonio, or maybe $700 to get to Los Angeles. Usually they demand a one-third down payment, followed by one-third at the border, and the balance at the destination. Most also offer a guarantee that includes repeated attempts until the migrant is successful.

Ranged against the coyotes are the 8,000 border patrol agents of the Immigration and Naturalization Service (INS), deploying high fences, night-sights, fast vehicles and helicopters. Whether this ultimately keeps people out is doubtful. More likely the increased INS enforcement in recent years has just diverted the coyotes and independent migrants to remoter and riskier crossing points. Over the period 1997-2000 around 700 people died, mostly by drowning, or by dehydration in the desert, though over the same period the INS says it rescued more than 2,000 people[16]. The INS also has 300 people on the Canadian border, which is twice as long but much less penetrated.

On average, the INS catches 1.5 million people annually. Most of these it just rounds up, loads onto buses and sends back to Mexico, giving them the opportunity to try again the next day. However, it also detains some people for deportation hearings. In this case it gives the best treatment to families with children – simply releasing them and requiring them to reappear for their hearing. Not surprisingly, this has created a market opportunity: many migrants 'rent' an assortment of children to bring with them just in case they get caught.

Smugglers also try to get migrants into the US by boat, particularly from the Caribbean. The most famous travelers by this route are Cubans, though they might consider themselves refugees rather than labor migrants. Their relatives in Miami can pay up to $8,000 for them to be smuggled in. In this case, the 'wet foot-dry foot' policy applies: if the travelers are apprehended at sea they are returned to Cuba, but if they manage to land in the US they are allowed to stay. For migrants from the Dominican Republic a favored route is via Puerto Rico, since Puerto Ricans have free entry into the United States. Smugglers charge around $500 to take people across the 120-mile (190-kilometer) Mona Passage to Puerto Rico on rickety boats called *yolas*. Many migrants drown or get eaten by sharks each year, either because the boats capsize or because the smugglers force them to swim ashore. Once in Puerto Rico, the migrants spend some time picking up false documents, as well as the local accent that will help them pass as Puerto Ricans.

For travelers coming to the US from further afield the journeys are more elaborate. The most sophisticated smugglers are the Chinese gangs known as 'snakeheads'. In recent years, they have been shipping migrants across the Pacific from Hong Kong to Los Angeles, for example, in cargo containers fitted with lights and fans that are powered by car batteries – and charging their clients around $60,000 each.

Other long-distance journeys have more complex, multi-legged itineraries with stopovers. One of these was revealed in 1998 when the INS arrested 21 members of an Indian gang that over a period of three years had smuggled in around 7,000 people, mostly Indians, for a fee of $20,000 per person. This involved three affiliated groups that passed people through Moscow to Cuba, then to Ecuador, the Bahamas or Mexico before taking them into the US at Texas, Florida and other points. The gang was eventually caught because of a dispute over payment. When some of their clients were apprehended the gang paid $5,000 each to bail them out but then added this to the $20,000 smuggling fee. Wrangling over this surcharge led to the tip-off[17]. Another hazard for those being transported long distances is that they may be abandoned en route, which often happens to Chinese migrants, who can find themselves stranded in Moscow or Bangkok.

For these expensive routes the smugglers generally demand that migrants repay the fares out of their subsequent wages, working in restaurants or sweatshops in New York or London. The gangs usually retain the immigrants' passports and other documents so that they cannot leave; in any case the gangs are so powerful, ruthless, and deeply rooted in the Chinese communities that it is difficult to escape their clutches. Even so, most migrants probably know what they are getting into, and are prepared to work for the two or three years that it will take to pay off the debt.

For smugglers hoping to get people into Europe the easiest routes are across the long and vulnerable land frontiers. The migrants may be Eastern Europeans wanting to get into Western Europe, or longer-distance travelers from Asia or Africa who are using Central and Eastern Europe as transit areas. The Chinese, for example, have visa-free entry into Yugoslavia. Once there, they then have many choices of entry to Western Europe, via the Czech Republic, for example, or Poland or Hungary.

Smuggling from China is now a well organized business particularly from the province of Fujian. From here a journey to the United States costs around $60,000; to the UK $45,000, or to Eastern Europe or Japan $12,000[18]. For those who want to reach the United Kingdom, the English Channel is a final hurdle. One of the most tragic incidents here was in June 2000 when 58 Chinese migrants were discovered at Dover to have suffocated to death while imprisoned in a container on a truck that had come through the Channel Tunnel. Since most smugglers rely on word-of-mouth recommendations they cannot afford such mistakes. The smuggler in Fujian responsible for that fateful trip reportedly had his house ransacked and was run out of town.

Smugglers also use more dangerous entries to Europe by sea – the 'blue routes'. From North Africa the most tempting crossing is the 12-mile (19-kilometer) trip across the Straits of Gibraltar – one of the world's most treacherous stretches of water. Until 1991 Spain allowed Moroccans to enter without visas as 'tourists', after which some would disappear. But under pressure from the European Union it started to require that Moroccans arrive only with visas. Soon Moroccans were paying up to $750 each to be smuggled across on fishing boats or, more dangerously, on the fragile, flat-bottomed *pateras* – ten- to thirteen-foot vessels that are normally used for in-shore fishing but which are now often crammed with 20 to 30 migrants.

The owners of these vessels prefer to avoid landing and often order their passengers to swim ashore through the strong currents. At least 200 people are thought to drown each year. In order to deter the crossings, the Spanish are installing a combined radar and infra-red 'electronic wall' along 350 miles (560 kilometers) of the southern coast. Now that Spanish patrol boats have become more vigilant, thousands of immigrants are opting for an alternative route, the 60-mile (96-kilometer) crossing to Lanzarote or Fuerteventura, the Canary Islands nearest to North Africa – a 20-hour trip by rowing boat. Most of the migrants using these routes are Moroccans or other North Africans, but there are also West Africans, particularly from Nigeria and Sierra Leone.

Other well-traveled sea routes into Europe are from Albania or Croatia to Italy. In this case the vessels are more robust. Some 200 high-powered speed boats ply the route from Vlore in Albania to Italy. Each carries around 30 passengers and covers the 40-mile (64-km) trip in an hour or so. The drivers do not hesitate to ram Italian customs vessels, or to dump their own passengers overboard when the going gets tough.

According to a Dutch organization, United for Inter-cultural Action, since 1993 1,574 people have died while trying to reach Europe. This includes those who have died while crossing rivers or seas, have frozen to death in refrigerated trucks, or have been suffocated by fumes in the holds of ferries[19]. However this only refers to documented cases and must be a considerable underestimate. Other estimates suggest a death toll two or three times higher.

In Asia and the Pacific, the borders tend to be more porous, so there is less need for physical smuggling. But for the harder countries such as Japan, migrants frequently travel with forged documents or arrive as tourists and overstay their visa. Many go via Bangkok which is a regional center for the production of high-quality forgeries that can even cope with the latest Japanese passport which has the owner's picture on the cover. Stolen Japanese passports are sent to Bangkok from all over the world and suitably amended. They cost around $2,000 each and are available from travel agents who advertise in the city's Chinese-language newspapers.

Trapped by the traffickers

Smuggling and trafficking are different activities but there is often considerable overlap between them, and the perpetrators may be the same people, so they are probably best thought of as opposite ends of a continuum[20]. Nevertheless it is important to try and maintain the distinction because the victims are otherwise likely to be treated as criminals.

There have been numerous attempts to define trafficking. One of the most recent definitions was produced as part of the UN Convention against Transnational Organized Crime, adopted by the General Assembly in November 2000. This states: *'Trafficking in persons' shall mean the recruitment, transportation, transfer, harboring or receipt of persons, by means of the threat or use of force or other forms of coercion, of abduction, of fraud, of deception, of the abuse of power or of a position of vulnerability …*[21].

Trafficking thus has one or two core components: coercion and deception. Coercion at its most serious involves kidnapping. A century ago this was a common way of getting workers. Chinese peasant farmers who might have come to Shanghai to sell vegetables were kidnapped and found themselves aboard a ship on the high seas – 'shanghaied'. Nowadays kidnapping is rare, though it does happen, chiefly to young women and children. Children from Eastern Europe and Africa have been kidnapped to work as prostitutes in Italy and other European countries. And there have also been stories of women from Mozambique being kidnapped and trafficked to South Africa to work as prostitutes. Within Central America, there are often accusations that children have been kidnapped from their parents before being sold for adoption.

Kidnapping is rare nowadays primarily because it is not necessary. There are easier ways of coercing victims. Some parents, for example, will abuse their authority over their children. In the southern provinces of Vietnam, some impoverished parents who are approached by traffickers will hand over their daughters in exchange for a small payment. The traffickers then take the children and sell them to brothels across the border in Cambodia. The girls have little or no say in this; still less when they are subsequently re-sold to other brothels. Similar things happen in Europe. In Germany, for example, there have been cases where children have been bought from Romanian parents and orphanages for around $500 each. They were smuggled first to Poland for training, then sent to German cities to work as pickpockets – and raped, beaten, cut with razor blades, and forced to eat their excrement if they did not cooperate or did not meet their daily targets. Later they were sold to other criminals for more than $10,000 each[22].

A more common form of trafficking is deception.

Sex trafficking in the Mekong Delta

The Mekong Delta Region is Asia's main focus for the trafficking of women for sex. Many women are moved to Thailand from neighboring countries, but others go from Thailand, Vietnam and Cambodia to Malaysia, Hong Kong, Taiwan and Japan. ∎

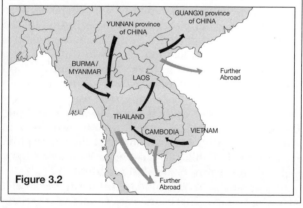

Figure 3.2

Again the victims voluntarily make a deal with the traffickers, only to find when they reach their destination that the work and conditions are very different from those they agreed to. Here the predominant activity is sex work. Young women and girls are told that there are opportunities for legitimate work overseas but discover on arrival that they are expected to offer sex. This happens all over the world but is particularly prevalent in Southeast Asia in the Mekong Delta – which comprises Cambodia, Laos, Burma, Thailand, Vietnam and the two southern Chinese provinces of Yunnan and Guangxi. The International Organization for Migration estimates that up to 300,000 women and children are trapped in 'slavery-like' conditions in the Mekong Delta'[23]. The main routes are indicated in figure 3.2. Traffickers lure girls to Thailand from Burma, Laos, Cambodia and the southern provinces of China. Most will get no further than Thai brothels, but Thailand has also become a regional hub – through which people are diverted to Malaysia, Hong Kong, Taiwan and Japan. Other important routes are from Vietnam into Cambodia and China.

Traffickers typically promise parents that they will find their daughters work in another country. Or they may make false promises to the child directly. In either case the girl is in for a shock when she realizes that she is expected to offer sexual services. At this point the brothel owner may physically force the girl to become a sex worker, often by locking her up and drugging her. Or the owner will simply tempt the girl with a large sum of money, offering $200 or more for her virginity. This presents the child with an intolerable dilemma. How can she turn down a sum that is more than her parents earn in a whole year, especially when the people who now surround her consider this normal and reasonable?[24] Most children in the Mekong region feel under an obligation to help their parents – a duty referred to in Thailand as 'repaying the breast-milk'. So a dutiful daughter may feel she is being disloyal to her parents if she refuses. Confused and frightened in a strange environment, it is not surprising that most eventually submit[25].

Similar forms of deception take place in the Philippines. Traffickers posing as talent agencies recruit women who want to go to Japan as entertainers, and may even give them training as singers or dancers, along with fake passports. But once in Japan the women are met by 'maintainers', frequently 'Yakuza' gang members, who often rape them before taking them to brothels or nightclubs.

By no means all women, or even children, who are moved from one country to another for sex work have been trafficked. Many are well aware of what they are getting into. The majority of adult sex workers specifically choose that occupation, even though they may have had limited options and acted out of desperation. Hervé Berger, manager of the ILO's regional project to combat trafficking in children and women in the Mekong region, says that only a small proportion of those recruited into illegal work, including prostitution, are being forced or deceived[26]. Probably the majority of sex workers who have moved to other countries have been smuggled rather than trafficked.

It is important to maintain this distinction – to single out trafficking as a specific crime – in order to protect the victims. Otherwise there is a danger that efforts to clamp down on illegal immigration or on prostitution will treat trafficking victims as criminals. The only practical way to prosecute traffickers is to use the testimony of victims. If the women fear that they will immediately be arrested and deported when they make a complaint there is little prospect of convicting the traffickers[27].

It is difficult to say how much trafficking is taking place. Since most of the activity is illegal it tends to elude regular systems of gathering statistics. United Nations' crime data, for example, do not include trafficking as a category[28]. One of the most commonly quoted estimates was made in 1994 by Jonas Widgren of the Vienna-based International Centre for Migration Policy and Development, who said that trafficking was a $6- to $7-billion business[29]. This statistic has been widely cited ever since, indeed few press features on trafficking fail to mention it[30]. And it has certainly served a very useful rhetorical purpose. But it involves a series of sometimes sweeping assumptions, so should be treated with caution.

However they travel, most migrants expect to find work at their destinations. Why are they so confident about this? And what effect does their arrival have on the workforce in the receiving country? That is the subject of the next chapter.

1 Massey, D. (1990). 'Social structure, household strategies, and the cumulative causation of migration', in *Population Index*, Vol. 56 No.1. **2** Glover, S., C. Gott, A. Loizillon, Portes, R. Price, S. Spencer, V. Srinivasan and C. Willis (2001). *Migration: An Economic and Social Analysis*. RDS Occasional Paper No 67. London, Home Office. **3** Jasso, G. and Rosenzweig, M. (1993). *Labor Immigration, Family Reunification, and Immigration Policy: The US experience*. Paper presented at the Conference on Migration and International Cooperation, Paris, OECD. **4** Dumon, W. (1989). 'Family and migration', *International Migration*, 28, No. 2. **5** NIDI/ Eurostat (2001). 'Why do people emigrate?', in *Statistics in Focus*, 1/2000. **6** Goza, F. (1994). 'Brazilian immigration to North America', in *International Migration Review* 28, n. 1. p. 44 **7** Light, Ivan, Parminder Bhachu, and Stavros Karageorgis (1993). *Migration Networks and Immigrant Entrepreneurship*. Available at: www.sscnet.ucla.edu/issr/paper/issr51.pdf. **8** Waldinger, R. (1996). 'The jobs immigrants take', in *The New York Times*, November 2. **9** Gray, Mark (2001). *Meatpacking and the migration of immigrant and refugee labor to Storm Lake, Iowa*. **10** Crisp, J. (1999). *Policy Challenges of the New Diasporas: Migrant Networks and their Impact on Asylum flows and Regimes*, New Issues in Refugee Research, Working Paper No. 7. Geneva, UNHCR. **11** *Weekly Mail and Guardian* (1998). *The major migrant networks*, Johannesburg. *Electronic Mail and Guardian,* September 14. **12** *Migration News* (2000). Vol. 7, No. 8, August. **13** Abella, M. (1995). *Policies and Institutions for the Orderly Movement of Labour Abroad*. International migration papers, no. 5, Geneva, ILO. **14** Jakarta Post (2001). '11 migrant workers taken hostage by labor export firm', in *Jakarta Post*, April 6. **15** *Migration News* (2001) Vol. 4, No. 4, April **16** *Migration News* (2000). Vol. 7, No. 7, July **17** *Migration News* (1998) Vol. 5, No. 12, December **18** Rosenthal, E. (2000) 'Chinese town's main export: its young men', in *New York Times*, June 26. **19** International

Choosing the destination

Organization for Migration (2000). 'Deaths in trafficking/smuggling' in *Trafficking in Migrants*, No. 21. **20** Salt, J. (2000). 'Trafficking and human smuggling: a European perspective', in *International Migration*, Vol. 38, No. 3. **21** United Nations (2000). General Assembly. Document A/55/383. Available at: www.undcp.org/palermo/convmain.html **22** ICMPD (1999). *The Relationship Between Organized Crime and Trafficking in Aliens*. A study prepared for the Budapest Group. **23** International Organization for Migration (1999). 'Turner Fund Trafficking Project' in *Trafficking in Migrants*, No. 20. **24** Duon Bach Le (1999). *Children in Prostitution in North Viet Nam: Rapid Assessment Findings*, ILO-IPEC South-East Asia Paper. **25** UNICEF (2001). *Every Last Child: Fulfilling the Rights of Women and Children in East Asia and the Pacific*. UNICEF East Asia and the Pacific Regional Office, Bangkok. **26** Ashayagachat, A. (2000). 'Gangs make Thailand a regional hub', in *Bangkok Post*, September 6 **27** UNICEF (2001). *Every Last Child: Fulfilling the Rights of Women and Children in East Asia and the Pacific*. UNICEF East Asia and the Pacific Regional Office, Bangkok. **28** Skinneder, E., Marcia Kran, Robert Adamson, and Ian Towsend-Gault (1997). 'Illegal labor movements and the trafficking of women: International dimensions in the era of globalization' in *Proceedings of the 1997 Regional Conference on Trafficking in Women and Children*. Bangkok, Mekong Regional Law Center. **29** Widgren, J. (1994). *International Response to Trafficking in Migrants and the Safeguarding of Migrant Rights*, paper presented at the 11th IOM Seminar on Migration, Geneva. **30** Stalker, P. (2000). 'Immigration deaths - Supply and demand, profit and peril', in *Sunday Herald*, Glasgow, June 25.

4 The economic benefits of immigration

The popular myth about immigrants is that they will 'take' something from the country they enter – that they will grab jobs or sponge off welfare systems. The reality is very different. Most industrial economies would be worse off without the help of immigrant workers, and without this injection of new blood the receiving countries will see their populations age and decline even more rapidly.

THE CRUDEST WAY of assessing the value of immigration is to look at the countries that have received large numbers of immigrants, and ponder whether this has done them much harm. The world's dominant economy, and one of the richest, is the United States – a country populated almost entirely by immigrants and their descendants. The US population has doubled over the last century, yet the country has become wealthier and wealthier. You could say the same of the other major countries of immigration, such as Australia and Canada – and make a similar case for South Africa which is by far Africa's richest country and remains a magnet for immigrants. In Asia the country with the highest proportion of immigrants – around one-quarter of the workforce – is Singapore, again one of the richest countries in the region. Within Europe, the country that has received the most immigrants in recent years is Germany, which has long been Europe's economic powerhouse. And the European countries with the largest proportions of immigrant workers, Switzerland and Luxembourg, are also the wealthiest. In fact, of the world's major industrial economies only Japan has not had significant influxes of migrant workers.

A statistical analysis for 15 European countries over the period 1991-95 found that for every 1 per cent increase in a country's population through immigration there was an increase in Gross Domestic Product of 1.25 to 1.5 per cent[1]. Of course this does not mean that immigration caused the increase in wealth – association is not the same as causation. And it could be argued that immigrants headed for such countries precisely because they were rich, and that without immigrants these countries would have been richer still. But would Germany be as wealthy without the energy of all its immigrant workers? Would the United States be better off if it had only 100 million people rather than 230 million? Highly unlikely. A more reasonable conclusion is that all these countries have not been held back by immigration but have used immigrants to become richer.

Putting immigrants to work

Some people who protest about immigration claim that immigrants are taking the jobs of native workers. At its most simplistic, this is based on the 'lump of labor fallacy' – a belief that the number of jobs in any country is fixed, so if more people come there will be fewer jobs to go round. This is clearly false. Each person creates work for others. So the larger the population the more the work that needs doing. People do not just take jobs, they also make jobs. The number of jobs and the rates of unemployment certainly go up and down, but these fluctuations have more to do with economic cycles and the structure of the economy. They have little relationship with population size or density. Indeed the richest countries are generally the ones that pack in the most people: in 1998 the world's highest population density was in Singapore, 5,186 people per square kilometer, where the per capita income was $30,000; the lowest population density was in Mongolia, with just two people per square kilometer, and a per capita income of $400[2].

It could be argued that this is a crude response to a crude proposition, and that the world is far more complex. Indeed it is. But it is important to bear in mind that adding more people, either by natural population increase or by immigration, does not necessarily reduce average national income, and may well increase it. This is not to say that the arrival of new workers has no impact on employment, but there is no reason why it should necessarily be negative, and many others to suggest that it is positive: that immigration makes the country as a whole richer.

You can see this effect kicking in as soon as immigrants step off the plane or the boat. They instantly create more work. First, they probably take a bus to their destination, which immediately provides more employment for bus drivers, other transport workers, or traffic police – as well as for the manufacturers of paper for bus tickets. Then they probably have breakfast – work for waiters, cooks, delivery drivers, farmers and sundry others. The problem for immigrants is that while the jobs they take are visible, the jobs they create for everyone else are largely invisible.

Then you need to look more closely at the jobs they take. Would native workers have done them otherwise? Not necessarily. The clearest indication of this is the flow of illegal workers. They have to find work – and fast – if they are not to spend all the cash in their pockets or exhaust the patience of the friends or relatives they live with. This means that they have to fill current vacancies. Not surprisingly, most immigrants choose destinations where the are confident they can find work immediately. In February 2000, a *Washington Post* reporter joined a dozen Mexicans who were about to cross the border clandestinely: 'All but one of them had jobs waiting: picking crops in Salinas, working construction in Los Angeles, washing dishes in a restaurant in Chicago'[3].

Professionals on the move

Migrants go to places that do not have enough local people with the skills or the willingness to do the jobs for the wages on offer. These vacancies tend to be concentrated at the top and the bottom of the skills spectrum. The newly industrializing countries in particular usually need more skilled people than their education systems can provide. Singapore, for example, has been one of the most aggressive recruiters of foreign professionals – around one fifth of its foreign workforce consists of doctors, teachers, accountants and myriad other professionals. But the countries of settlement have also gone out of their way to recruit skilled people. The United States in 2000 had 420,000 foreign professionals – people granted the H-1B visas to fill jobs where there is no suitable local candidates[4]. Australia too has tried to attract more skilled workers and has recently increased the number of people who can come in under the highly-skilled category.

Canada has been even more determined to recruit skilled people. In 1998 almost half of immigrants were skilled workers and their accompanying dependants. The effect was evident in the 1996 census which found that of the 25- to 44-year-olds who had arrived since 1991 more than one-third had completed university education, compared with only 19 per cent for people born in Canada. Unfortunately for Canada, the country also suffers an exodus of professionals to the United States: in 1993-94, this was the equivalent of 14 per cent of the doctors and scientists who had been produced by Canada's education system[5].

European countries are again trying to attract skilled immigrants. The Federation of German Employers said in 2000 that Germany was short of 1.5 million skilled workers. In May 2000, Germany announced a new scheme to allow in 30,000 non-EU foreign computer professionals who would have five-year work visas on salaries of a minimum of $47,000 a year – though this proposal met with some opposition and had to be scaled down[6]. By the end of January 2000, only 5,000 workers had arrived, mostly from Eastern Europe rather than from India[7]. Nevertheless, the demand remains.

In the United Kingdom the immigrant population is weighted towards professionals, who make up 30 per cent of the foreign population compared with 25 per cent for the national population[8]. But even this is not enough to meet the demand, particularly in information technology and health care: in mid-2000, the National Health Service was short of around 17,000 nurses. The British government has therefore started to ease the restrictions on the issue of work permits[9].

3-D employment

At the other end of the skill spectrum are the millions of unskilled workers – the day laborers, the fruit-pickers, the factory hands, the office cleaners – everyone who does the 3-D 'dirty, dangerous and difficult work'. As Chapter 2 indicated, this reflects a 'dual labor market' based on a core of permanent well-paid workers, who are complemented by a larger number of temporary or contract workers, most of whom are less skilled.

But there are also powerful social forces at work here. Many national workers have been conditioned to reject the 3-D jobs. In the industrial countries, the proportion of the population opting for tertiary education – university or college – has risen dramatically in recent decades. Along with the expansion of the middle class in most countries, this has squeezed the proportion of manual workers. This applies not just to unskilled workers, but also to skilled manual workers. As more young people opt for cleaner, white-collar work, far fewer want to become apprenticed to skilled trades. Denmark, for example, estimates that it will replace only half the skilled bricklayers and masons who will retire in the next decade[10]. In Canada too the construction industry is worried that the majority of skilled workers are now in their forties or fifties. These are the gaps that immigrants are filling. In France, foreigners are only 7 per cent of workers but are over 15 per cent of those employed in construction[11]. In the UK immigrants account for around 70 per cent of people working in London's catering industry.

One alternative is to raise salaries to attract native workers. But employers are reluctant to do this, particularly when they can employ immigrants. In Germany in 1996 unemployment was above 12 per cent, and there were around 200,000 unemployed construction workers. Meanwhile Germany had welcomed around 500,000 foreign construction workers. Not all were from Turkey or Morocco or Eastern Europe. Around 100,000 were from the United Kingdom, attracted by the high salaries. At home British construction workers might have been getting £8 ($12) per hour, but in Germany they could get $25. The employers were happy with this since the equivalent German workers, even at the minimum wage, would cost $35 per hour. Moreover, they found that the British immigrants, who were away from home and had little else to do, were happy to take as many overtime shifts as they were offered.

The 3-D immigrant workers are generally lower down the wage and status ladder than national workers. But there are also distinctions between immigrants, often depending on the country they come from. Most receiving countries have a hierarchy of immigrants and give the most unpopular jobs to the least-favored nations. In the Netherlands, for example, the immigrants at the top of the pile are those from the Netherlands Antilles – Caribbean islands that make up a Dutch dependency that has benefited from large-scale Dutch aid. People from these islands can enter the Netherlands freely. They speak either Dutch or English and are typically well educated, so they do more or less the same work as the general population. Indonesians too tend to have better jobs since most have been in the country a long time. Lower down the scale are more recent arrivals from the former colony of Suriname. Although they too speak Dutch, they are not so well educated and mostly work in industry and services – often doing clerical tasks. At the bottom of the pile are workers from Turkey and Morocco, most of whom are doing unskilled or semi-skilled jobs in industry[12]. These differences are also reflected in unemployment rates. In 1998 in the Netherlands the unemployment rate for EU nationals and for Indonesians was 5 per cent, but for workers from Suriname it was 17 per cent, and for those from Turkey it was 28 per cent.

The same issues emerge all over the world as standards of education – and aspirations – rise. The Republic of Korea has had persistent labor shortages for decades but has tried to avoid using official immigrant labor. A survey by the ILO and the Korean Institute of Labor in the early 1990s among small and medium-sized firms found a vacancy rate of around 9 per cent, yet employers were still unwilling to raise wages for jobs at the bottom of the wage ladder since this would push up all the other wages. The Korean government wants more women and old people either to start working or to return to work. But most of the firms say this is impractical for heavy physical work. In any case they find that Koreans refuse to do even the lighter work for the wages on offer[13].

Meanwhile the construction, laboring and cleaning jobs still need doing. In South Korea this happens in two main ways. The first is through a system of 'trainees' – people supposedly brought in to learn new skills, but actually used largely as manual labor, chiefly in factories making textiles, electronics, chemicals, toys and musical instruments. In 1999 South Korea had around 98,000 trainees. Their pay was fixed at $576 per month – less than the minimum wage, and they were not covered by Korean labor laws. Not surprisingly, most trainees rapidly abandon the companies to which they have been assigned and 'go illegal'. The second main way of meeting the labor shortage in Korea is to employ illegal immigrants.

South Korea is a difficult place to sneak into; border controls are very tight, so most illegals are people who arrived legally but are overstaying their visas – the majority from China, Mongolia, Bangladesh and the Philippines. In 1999 Korea had 135,000 'visa overstayers' who were either taking exceptionally long holidays or working illegally. Although the Asian economic crisis temporarily reduced the demand for workers, by 2000 the total number of legal and illegal immigrants had climbed back to pre-crisis levels.

Japan is in a comparable position and adopts similar subterfuges. During its period of rapid economic expansion Japan resisted employing foreign workers in manufacturing industry, preferring instead to relocate production overseas. But the country still has many jobs in construction and services that it cannot export. It fills some of these through legal immigration, notably of women; of the 102,000 people that Japan admitted in 1998 with restricted permission to work, 74,000 were female 'entertainers' from the Philippines and Thailand. The other vacancies are filled unofficially. Japan also has 280,000 visa overstayers. In addition there are 28,000 students in Japanese-language schools who are also allowed to work, along with 50,000 'trainees' – young people earning around $800 per month, working mostly as unskilled laborers and learning very little. As in Korea, trainees in Japan are tempted to escape to better-paid jobs on construction sites, though their employers frequently keep their passports in order to stop them absconding.

Foreign laborers are found on construction sites all over the world. In Argentina, for example, construction workers are typically from Chile and Brazil, earning up to ten times more than they can at home[14]. Bolivian laborers also enter Argentina but they are more likely to take jobs in agriculture, working their way down the country according to the seasons – cutting sugar cane and picking oranges in the northern provinces, then moving to vineyards further south, and later in the year working on potato farms near Buenos Aires or picking apples in the flatlands near Patagonia.

An alternative to immigration is mechanization. To some extent this has been possible in farming. Sugar cane, for example, which in many countries is cut by machete, can also be cut by machine. In Florida in the mid-1990s, harvesting machines eventually displaced thousands of Jamaican immigrant cane cutters. But it is more difficult to mechanize the harvesting of delicate soft fruit and even some vegetables. The booming strawberry industry in California, for example, has created thousands of jobs for immigrants – a phenomenon that has been referred to as the 'Mexicanization rather than mechanization' of US agriculture. The harvesting of mushrooms is also highly labor intensive. One of the main mushroom-growing areas in the United States is Southern Chester County, Pennsylvania. Because local people here have always been reluctant to harvest mushrooms the work has been taken by successive waves of immigrants. First they were Italians; later they were poor whites from Tennessee and West Virginia, and blacks from South Carolina; then they were Puerto Ricans; and nowadays they are Mexicans, many of them undocumented. If anything, mushroom harvesting has become even more labor intensive: previously the workers just used to pull out the mushrooms, now they have to cut them carefully to retain the 'eye appeal' that supermarkets demand[15].

Many governments argue that admitting immigrants just delays mechanization and slows the transition towards higher-tech production, whether in agriculture, industry or services. In Malaysia, for example, where petrol pumps used to be largely operated by Bangladeshi attendants, the government decreed in 1997 that all pumps would have to convert to self-service – though it would still have been far cheaper to keep Bangladeshis working around the clock. More

recently the Malaysian government has also been trying to encourage mechanization in the rubber and
palm-oil plantations.

Smoothing the peaks and troughs

One advantage of using immigrants, particularly if
they are undocumented, is that they can readily be
hired and fired – brought in to meet sudden demands
for labor and then dismissed when surplus to require-
ments. This is most obvious for seasonal agricultural
laborers who are only needed at harvest time. But construction also has peaks and troughs, and runs largely
on a casual basis with immigrant laborers moving from
one building site to the next.

Receiving countries may also attempt to smooth out
peaks that stretch over longer periods – years or even
decades. Capitalism has inbuilt tendencies towards
boom and bust. This means that employers want lots
of workers at the peak of the economic cycle but find
they have too many when the economy sinks into
recession. During the 1960s and early 1970s this is
what encouraged Germany to attract millions of 'guest
workers'. Fully aware that they might not be needed in
a few years the German government gave the guest
workers one- or two-year work permits. German trade
unions, who were closely involved in the whole opera-
tion, did not object. They secured an agreement that
first preference would always be given to Germans and
that immigrants would be paid decent wages so they
could not undercut native workers.

This proved a very successful strategy that not only
provided jobs for immigrants but also created better
opportunities for native workers: a number of studies
have shown that immigration allowed more German
workers to take on better-paid professional jobs. When
boom did turn to bust in 1973 it proved very difficult
to force out many of the guest workers who by then
had put down roots. Nevertheless it has been argued
that even in later years Germany's GDP would have

impossible to get a green card for a nanny
e worker. As one immigration lawyer told
Times: "If you start the green-card process
by sitter now, she'd be eligible to care
your grandchildren". The most likely
richer families is to employ one of the
airs[21].

aid immigrant minds the children this can
educated and skilled mother to work as a
ed executive. But the nanny herself may
hly educated. Many teachers or other pro-
eave the Philippines because they cannot
or because even professional jobs do not
. When they come to Europe or the United
may be earning more, but working as
ducated immigrant women also work as
ervants in Latin America: in Argentina in
cumenical Support Service for Immigrants
ees interviewed 80 Paraguayan, Peruvian
an women and discovered that two-thirds of
working as domestic servants even though
ost-secondary-school degrees[22].

even more true of those who arrive as
In the United Kingdom, research by the
ice found that one-third of all those accept-
ees had university degrees, or post-graduate
ional qualifications: 'There were academics,
il servants, doctors, accountants, teachers,
ngineers, businesspeople, managers, mem-
e armed forces, office workers, nurses ....'[23]
even when they are allowed to work many
ind that their foreign degrees or other qual-
are not recognized in their new country, so
till finish up washing dishes.
e cases the availability of an immigrant may
se native workers for less valuable functions.
ed Kingdom has been recruiting many more
d teachers overseas. Trade unions argue that
em in the UK is not that there are no local

grown more slowly without the immigrants[16].

The Asian financial crisis from 1997 also de
strated the use of migrant workers as shock absorbers.
Malaysia was probably the immigration country hard-
est hit by the crisis and the government made
determined efforts to reduce the number of migrant
workers, who make up around one-quarter of the
workforce. The government stepped up security to
prevent the arrival of new immigrants, stopped issuing
new work permits, and refused to renew many existing
ones. As a result of these and other measures, the
number of registered foreign workers declined by an
estimated 23 per cent in 1998 and by a further 20 per
cent in 1999. There was also a fall in the number of
illegal workers – by around 10 per cent in 1998. By the
end of 1998 it was becoming clear, however, that the 5
per cent of the national workforce still unemployed
had no desire to work on rubber plantations or building sites, so the government had to ease the
restrictions. Thailand had a similar experience. At the
outset of the financial crisis, the Thai government
tried to expel thousands of workers from Burma,
Cambodia and Laos, but Thais nowadays are choosier
about the work they will do, so the Thai government
eventually had to backtrack – opting instead to issue
one-year work permits to illegal immigrants.

The major receiving countries also try to adjust the
arrival of immigrants to reflect current demands.
Canada has been quite adroit at turning the immigration tap on and off according to economic
circumstances. Figure 4.1 overleaf illustrates the ensu-
ing switchback ride[17]. At certain points, notably the
1930s and early 1940s, more people emigrated than
immigrated[18].

Keeping old industries afloat

Governments may want to force enterprises to auto-
mate, but there are many companies, particularly
smaller ones, for whom this is just too expensive. If they

Canada's immigration tap

Canada has a sophisticated 'points system' for immigration and turns the tap on and off to meet its immediate needs for workers. During several periods, more people have emigrated than immigrated. ■

Figure 4.1 – Canada, immigration and emigration, 1970-96

cannot find native workers they must employ immigrants or go out of business. These industries will probably die eventually, but in the meantime immigrant labor helps keep them afloat – and sustains employment for supervisors and managers and for people working in all the ancillary businesses. The classic sunset industries in the richer countries are textiles and garments. From 18th-century Great Britain onwards, almost all countries have embarked on industrialization with textiles and garments. The technology is simple, and in the case of garments fairly labor intensive. And there is always a ready market: people everywhere need clothes, and the more they earn the more clothes they buy. First in Europe, then in the United States, then in East Asia, industrialization was kick-started with garments. Later these countries moved on to more sophisticated products, not least because they faced competition from younger and hungrier economies. As a result, over the past few

decades the centre of grav
has shifted to developing c
1994 their share of the g
clothing rose from 21 per c
  Nevertheless the garmer
certain extent in richer
because of tariff protectio
have been able to boost the
has a very sophisticated sy
small producers, has been
Another factor is that segr
always be embedded in the
ish end of the clothing indu
to respond to sudden chang
ufacturers prefer stay close t
That is one reason why New
a significant garment industr
Europe as elsewhere much
industry, even in high fashior
labor, via a network of cont
tors. So a garment that migh
for $50 from a designer, who
it for $30 who gets a sub-cont
who pays a worker to make it

Making better use of native

Another way that immigrants
and income of natives is by rel
er-paid jobs. The clearest ex
immigrants to look after child
ically mothers, can go out
countries nowadays have a fa
women working. And more wo
– or would work longer hour
affordable child care. The be
pay nannies, but most have to
ters. The United States has
workers but pay is low, less tha
McDonalds, and turnover is hig

it is almost
or a day-ca
the New Yo
for your k
legally fo
option for
11,000 au
  If a low-
release an
high-powe
also be his
fessionals
find work
pay enoug
States the
cleaners.
domestic
2000 the
and Refu
and Boliv
them wer
they had
  This is
refugees.
Home O
ed as refu
or profes
senior ci
lawyers,
bers of t
However
refugees
ification:
they can
  In sor
also rele
The Uni
nurses a
the prol

people to do the work, it is just that they are not prepared to do it for the low wages on offer. In this case you might get an Australian primary school teacher coming to fill a vacancy in London created because a British teacher can earn more working as an estate agent. Whether this constitutes making better use of native workers is debatable.

Do immigrants depress the wages of local workers?

When economies are booming and businesses are crying out for workers it is easier to see that immigrants are valuable. But what happens if the immigrants keep coming even during an economic slow-down when there is widespread unemployment? Even then, many of the underlying advantages of employing immigrants remain. Immigrants are still consumers who create work for others – particularly those working in professional jobs. And they will still do work that others reject: few business managers or electricians or shop assistants who are made redundant are prepared to step out of the front door the next day to work as building laborers or street cleaners. Most would prefer to take unemployment benefit or even stop working altogether.

This is just as well. The unemployment insurance system is not simply designed to allow the unemployed to survive; it also makes capitalism run more smoothly. In all industrial economies old industries die off while new businesses constantly surface to take their place. This means that skilled workers who are made redundant will need time to seek out the best job, learning new skills if necessary. Indeed one of the handicaps for developing countries is precisely that they do not have unemployment insurance. If a skilled factory worker in Jakarta is made redundant, he or she cannot afford to be out of work, so becomes a street vendor, or starts strumming a guitar at traffic lights, or goes back to the family farm. In industrial countries, professionals in many fields are often prepared to make hundreds of applications, hanging on until they find the precise job that makes best use of their talents – a type of job matching that is only possible because of unemployment benefit.

One of the simplest ways of investigating whether immigration adds to unemployment during a recession is to compare two periods of time and see if an increase in immigration is matched by an increase in unemployment. The Paris-based Organization for Economic Cooperation and Development (OECD) has carried out this exercise for a range of countries for the periods 1984-89 and 1990-95[24]. The results are shown in table 4.1 and indicate no relationship at all between the growth in immigrant arrivals: in the countries that had the highest inflows of immigrants unemployment often stayed the same or went down.

There have also been a number of more precise investigations of the effect of immigration on jobs and wages for individual countries. The overall conclusion is that the arrival of more immigrants has little or no effect on unemployment and wages for the country as a

Table 4.1 – Gross immigration inflows and unemployment in selected OECD countries

	1984-89 Average Inflows '000s	Unemployment rate, %	1990-95 Average gross Inflows '000s	Unemployment rate, %	% point difference in unemployment rates
United States	675	6.4	1,128	6.4	0.0
Germany	520	7.6	920	8.1	+0.5
Japan	183	2.6	284	2.5	-0.1
Switzerland	69	0.7	101	2.9	+2.2
France	45	10.0	93	10.7	+2.2
United Kingdom	50	8.6	54	9.4	+0.8
Norway	18	3.0	18	5.5	+2.5
Luxembourg	7	1.6	10	2.0	+0.4

SOPEMI (1997)

Notes: Data for Germany are for West Germany until 1990, and subsequently for Germany as a whole.

whole, though in some countries certain groups may have benefited more while others could marginally have lost out.

The United States

One way of assessing the impact of immigration in the United States is to compare cities that have had large influxes of immigrants, like New York or Los Angeles, with other cities like Nashville or Pittsburgh that have been less popular destinations. US economists have carried out a whole raft of studies of this type, looking at the impact of immigration on three groups of workers: whites, Hispanics and blacks. All come to very similar conclusions – that any effect either way has been very slight[25]. They found that the only group that seemed to lose out generally from new arrivals were the previous cohort of immigrants[26].

Another way of judging the impact is to see what happens in one location before and after a sudden influx. One opportunity occurred in April 1980 when Fidel Castro declared that many Cubans who wished to do so could leave Cuba from the port of Mariel. Over the next six months around 125,000 people, mostly unskilled workers and their families, set off for Florida. This 'Mariel flow' increased the labor force in Miami by 7 per cent yet seemed to have little or no effect on employment or wages for the local population[27].

One reason why immigrants might not have much effect on local wages, however, is that national workers might leave the area when immigrants arrive – or at least be dissuaded from moving there because they think they will be competing for work with immigrants. This may have been happening in California, which has been attracting high-income whites and low-income immigrants, while it has been losing low-income whites. But even here these effects seem to be very slight.

In its 1997 report to Congress, the US Commission on Immigration Reform reviewed the most recent evidence in a study from the National Academy of

Sciences (NAS)[28]. This found that immigrants added up to $10 billion to the US economy each year – though this is a very slight effect on a $10-trillion economy, equivalent to around one week's usual growth. The native workers who benefited most were those whose skills were complementary to those of immigrants and those who were working in industries such as garments or shoemaking that might otherwise have disappeared.

The report also found that many immigrant entrepreneurs created employment for native workers by trading with their countries of origin, while immigrant employees were able to use their language skills and contacts to benefit US exporters. The NAS found that the groups that were most likely to lose out from immigration were recent immigrants and also the lowest-skilled Americans, particularly high-school drop-outs, who found it more difficult to compete with the new arrivals, and who nationwide are thought to have suffered a 5 per cent drop in wages.

Australia

There has also been a lot of research in Australia on the economic impact of immigration – understandable in a country where immigrants make up around one-fifth of the labor force. Here the conclusion has consistently been that immigrants create at least as many jobs as they occupy. This has been true even during periods of recession.

The Bureau of Immigration Policy Research, for example, looked at immigration during the recessions of 1974-75, 1982-83, and 1992-93 and found no relationship between immigration and unemployment. Moreover, those who benefited most from the new jobs were the Australian born[29]. Since then Australia has been attempting to further increase the skill levels of its immigrants, with the result that immigration over the period 2000-05 is expected to add $260 to the country's per capita income[30].

Canada

Here too the conclusion has been that immigrants are not competing with the national population. In 1991, for example, the Economic Council of Canada concluded that a steady level of immigration, high or low, does not lead to unemployment, since the number of firms simply increases, creating corresponding new jobs[31]. Other studies have come to similar conclusions, saying that while specific groups may face extra competition from immigrants, there is little or no impact on the workforce as a whole[32].

Europe

There have been far fewer investigations of the employment effect of immigration in Europe, partly because many European countries in principle do not consider they are countries of immigration. Some investigations in Germany, similar to those in the United States, have compared cities with high and low proportions of immigrants, and found that the arrival of immigrants made little or no difference[33]. Other investigations concluded that immigrants have expanded opportunities for the German population[34], though some researchers suggest that some blue-collar workers might have lost out[35]. In the UK there have been few studies on the effect on immigration on employment, but their conclusions largely confirm the US pattern. One study finds that a 1 per cent increase in immigrant labor has only a very small effect on the wages of UK-born workers (between +0.02 per cent and –0.08 per cent)[36].

There have also been some investigations in Europe, looking at the impact of a sudden influx of immigrants. One in Portugal assessed the effect of the repatriation from Angola of 600,000 *retornados* – Portuguese settlers who returned home in the mid-1970s when Portugal hastily disposed of its colonial possessions. Comparisons of Portugal's experience with that of Spain and France over the same period, concluded that if there was any effect on native employment it had been very slight[37].

Since immigrants are often working in the least stable and lowest-paid jobs they do however, typically have higher levels of unemployment than native workers. In the UK in 2001, for example, when the unemployment rate for the UK born was just under 5 per cent it was 6 per cent for the foreign born. However the contrast is much greater elsewhere. In France where unemployment is around 11 per cent it is over 30 per cent for non-EU immigrants[38].

Immigrants and the welfare state

Apart from taking the jobs of native workers, immigrants are also frequently accused of coming to a richer country simply to sponge off the state. Here the issue is whether immigrants are likely to receive more in terms of benefits – health care, social security, and education – than they contribute in taxes.

Welfare for immigrants has been something of a statistical battleground in the United States. There are, for example, different definitions of what constitutes welfare – should you include only cash payments, or should you include school lunches for poor children? There are also disputes about who counts as an immigrant. If an immigrant's child who was born in the United States – and is therefore a native US citizen – receives Medicaid, some would regard that as welfare going to an 'immigrant household'. Taking the unit of measurement to be the person rather than the household, and counting all US-born children as 'natives', then data for the early 1990s suggest that the proportion of the native born receiving cash benefits is 4.9 per cent while the proportion for immigrants is marginally higher at 6.6 per cent[39]. For Medicaid, the proportions are 7.3 per cent and 8.6 per cent – close to a statistical margin of error.

The overall picture seems to be therefore that immigrants in the US make slightly more use of welfare than do natives. But this is mainly because immigrants are on average poorer than natives. In fact if you look specifically at low-income families, then low-income immigrants are less likely to claim welfare than low-income natives[40]. Critics of immigration argue that this is precisely the problem: that the United States is now letting in too many lower-skilled people who are poorer and thus more likely to need welfare. Worries about immigrants' use of welfare resulted in the 1996 Welfare Reform Act which imposed broad new restrictions on legal immigrants' access to public benefits. All new immigrants are now barred from receiving federal means-tested public benefits for at least five years.

Legal immigrants can eventually claim welfare, but that option in theory at least is not open to illegal immigrants. Some will have already acquired false documents, such as birth certificates, social security cards and even fake 'green cards' in order to get work. So they might also be able to get forged documentation for claiming welfare. But there is no evidence that this is actually happening. Most researchers believe that illegal immigrants are so preoccupied with concealing their existence and their whereabouts from the authorities that the last thing they would do would be to claim welfare. In that case, they are making a net contribution to the state and federal coffers. Employers who treat them as legal immigrants will be withholding federal income tax and paying social security taxes to the government. As a result, some calculations suggest that undocumented immigrants are paying five to ten times more in taxes than they are consuming in welfare services[41].

The issue of the use of government services by immigrants came to a head in 1994 when 59 per cent of those voting in California supported 'proposition 187' which, among other things, would have denied education to the children of illegal immigrants. This might seem reasonable, since the children are not supposed to be there. But it takes a rather narrow view of the purpose of education. Most people regard schooling not as a welfare benefit to an individual child but as an essential investment in the future of the society. Since many undocumented immigrant families are likely to stay, and in the long term to become citizens, keeping their children illiterate does not sound like a good way to keep them off the welfare rolls. Fortunately, proposition 187 was annulled by the courts in 1999 before it could be enacted.

Taking the longer view of immigration, the US National Academy of Sciences has concluded that although immigrants will in the early years add to costs, particularly for education, eventually each immigrant, with his or her descendants paying taxes, will make a net positive contribution to the national budget of $80,000. This is illustrated in figure 4.2[42] which follows the effect on the state and federal budgets of an immigrant arriving in 1994. This shows the net balance turning positive after 20 years or so.

The other countries of immigration have also looked at the use of welfare by immigrants and have

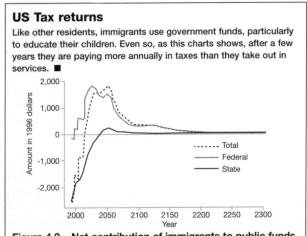

US Tax returns

Like other residents, immigrants use government funds, particularly to educate their children. Even so, as this charts shows, after a few years they are paying more annually in taxes than they take out in services. ■

Figure 4.2 – Net contribution of immigrants to public funds

Smith and Edmondson (1997)

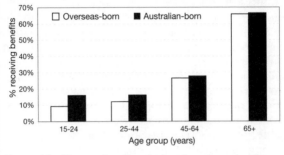

Birrell and Jupp (2000)

Behind in benefits

Immigrants to Australia, particularly when they are younger, make less use of welfare benefits, such as unemployment or disability benefit, than do the Australian-born. But they catch up as they grow older, especially after retirement. ■

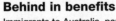

Figure 4.3 – Usage of welfare by immigrants and native Australians

concluded that they are more than paying their way. This was confirmed in an Australian study in 2000 which found that for the younger age groups in particular immigrants were less likely to be receiving welfare payments than the Australian-born[43]. The results are presented in figure 4.3. For those aged 15-24, 9 per cent of immigrants were receiving benefits compared with 16 per cent for the Australian-born. The same research also found that immigrants' usage of welfare declined over time. Thus for those aged 25-44 the proportion of welfare usage was 17 per cent for those who had arrived during the period 1991-96, compared with 11 per cent for those who had arrived during the period 1986-90.

In the United Kingdom a recent analysis suggests that immigrants contribute far more in taxes and National Insurance than they consume in benefits and other public services. The foreign-born population contributes around 10 per cent more government revenue than they take in benefits. Indeed, were it not for the immigrant population either public services would have to be cut or the government would need to increase the basic rate of income tax by one penny in the pound[44].

Running out of people

Some Europeans claim that their countries do not have room for immigrants. But with family sizes falling the likelihood is that without immigration European populations will start to shrink. Birth rates have been falling for many reasons, but chiefly because more women are choosing to work, and to have fewer children – or none at all. The average number of children that each woman has in her lifetime is termed the 'total fertility rate'. For the population to keep stable, assuming that death rates remain the same and that there is no net immigration, the fertility rate needs to be 2.2 children per woman – which is termed the 'replacement rate'. If you look at table 4.2 below you will see that none of these countries is replacing its population quickly enough. For the European Union as a whole the fertility rate is down to around 1.4[45].

All these countries face population decline. This

Table 4.2 – Fertility rates in selected countries					
	1950-1955	1965-1970	1995-2000	2020-2025	2045-2050
France	2.7	2.6	1.7	2.0	2.0
Germany	2.2	2.3	1.3	1.6	1.6
Italy	2.3	2.5	1.2	1.5	1.7
Japan	2.8	2.0	1.4	1.7	1.8
South Korea	5.4	4.7	1.7	1.9	1.9
Russian Federation	2.5	2.0	1.4	1.7	1.7
UK	2.2	2.5	1.7	1.9	1.9
United States	3.5	2.6	2.0	1.9	1.9
Europe	2.6	2.4	1.4	1.7	1.8
European Union	2.4	2.5	1.4	1.5	1.8

United Nations Population Division (2000)

will not happen immediately since the higher birth rates of the 1960s have helped sustain population momentum. But eventually populations will fall. Italy will have the steepest decline: between 2000 and 2050 the population will fall from 57 million to 41 million. And Japan's population will fall from 127 million to 105 million. The decline in the UK over this period will be a little gentler – from 59 million to 56 million.

Is this a problem? Environmentalists argue that a shrinking population in a rich country is a good thing: the fewer people the better, though quite how few they would prefer is not clear. Nationalists, on the other hand, will be dismayed since they regard a large economy and population as a symbol of national virility. Those wanting a compromise can opt for 'zero population growth', though the justification for this is not obvious, apart from an irrational preference for round numbers.

But there is a further issue apart from the size of the population, and that is its age structure. If the population is falling because fewer children are being born, as well as because more people are living longer, then the population as a whole is 'graying'. In 1950 only 12 per cent of the population of the more developed

Table 4.3 – Potential support ratio, assuming zero net migration after 1995

	1950	1975	2000	2025	2050
France	5.8	4.7	4.1	2.8	2.3
Germany	6.9	4.3	4.1	2.5	1.8
Italy	7.9	5.3	3.7	2.4	1.5
Japan	12.1	8.6	4.0	2.2	1.7
South Korea	18.2	16.3	10.7	4.4	2.4
Russian Federation	10.5	7.7	5.5	3.6	2.4
United Kingdom	6.2	4.5	4.1	2.9	2.4
United States	7.8	6.2	5.2	3.1	2.6
Europe	8.0	5.7	4.7	3.0	2.0
European Union	7.0	4.8	4.1	2.7	1.9

United Nations Population Division (2000)

The economic benefits of immigration

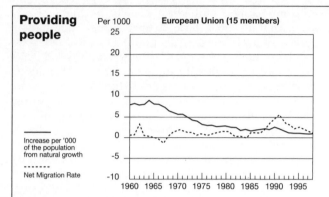

Providing people

Immigration has steadily become more significant in sustaining population levels in the UK and the countries of European Union – as natural population growth rates have fallen to zero or below. ∎

SOPEMI (2000)

regions was over 65; by 2000 the proportion was 19 per cent ; and by 2050 it is going to be 33 per cent[46]. This means that there are going to be fewer people of working age supporting the non-working population. The dependants include both the young and the old, but the old are more expensive: it costs around two and a half times more to support an older person (aged 65 or above) than to support a young person (under 20 years of age)[47].

Most countries will want to increase the number of working people per pensioner – to maximize the 'support ratio'. The long-term outlook is indicated in table 4.3 which shows that without net immigration (more people arriving than leaving) support ratios are going to halve over the next 50 years. Few 20 year-olds spend much time pondering their pension. But if you are 20 or so at the beginning of the 21st century, and you do think about it, prepare to worry.

Could immigration offer a solution? Certainly it can help sustain overall numbers. For the UK, for example, it has been estimated that without immigration from the Commonwealth after the Second World War the

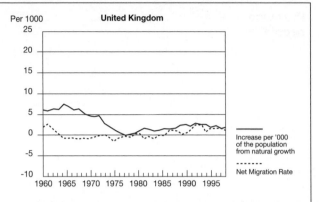

Figure 4.4 – Immigration and natural growth rates in the EU and the UK

population by the 1990s would have been around 5 per cent smaller. For the industrial countries as a whole, between 1990 and 1995 immigration was responsible for around 45 per cent of all population growth, and for most countries this proportion has been rising. This is illustrated for the countries of the European Union and for the UK in figure 4.4, in which the solid line is the increase, per thousand, of the population from natural growth (births minus deaths), and the dotted line is the net migration rates (immigration minus emigration), again per thousand of the total population. As you can see, the contribution from natural growth has been falling while that from immigration has held steady – apart from the peak in the early 1990s which corresponds to the break-up of the Soviet Union and migration to Germany. In the UK, net migration has frequently been negative.

For the countries of settlement the pattern is somewhat different, though not necessarily what you might expect. In Australia and the United States, all the rates are higher (figure 4.5 overleaf) and in this case natural growth exceeds net immigration. However, this is

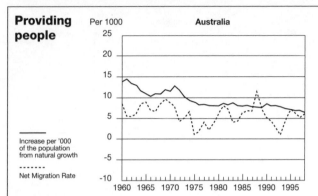

Providing people

Per 1000

Australia

Increase per '000 of the population from natural growth

------- Net Migration Rate

1960 1965 1970 1975 1980 1985 1990 1995

The countries of large-scale immigration, such as the United States and Australia, have higher natural population growth rates, but this is primarily because immigrant families also tend to have more children. ■

SOPEMI (2000)

also the result of immigration: immigrants generally have larger families than the native population, so once they are within the country births within their families are counted as part of natural growth.

Immigrants tend to rejuvenate the population because the people most likely to emigrate are the young. In Canada in 1986, for example, the average age of immigrants was 27 years while that for the population as a whole was 32. The young have had less time to acquire many ties in their own country, and since it costs money to travel, they will have more time to recoup the investment. Moreover, the young are also more adventurous and will be looking for new horizons.

Immigrants also rejuvenate the host population because they have larger families. Turkish immigrant women in Sweden, for example, tend to have more children than native Swedes. Partly this is cultural, since immigrants mostly come from countries where people are accustomed to having larger families. The total fertility rate in Turkey is 2.5 while in Sweden it is only 1.7[48]. So you would expect Turkish immigrants to

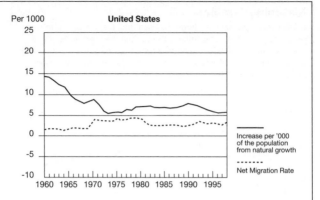

Figure 4.5 – Immigration and natural growth rates in Australia and the United States

have more children than native Swedish women. Another issue is income: immigrants are often poorer than the average for the host country, and poorer families generally have more children.

Nevertheless, immigrants soon start to pick up the habits of their host countries. And the longer they stay, the more likely they are to want smaller families. In France, for example, a comparison was made of the fertility patterns of immigrants who arrived over the period 1975-82 with immigrants of the same nationality who were already in place. In the case of Algerian women the new arrivals had fertility rates of 5.9 children, while for women in the existing Algerian immigrant community in France the fertility rate was only 3.7. The same was true for other nationalities: Italians, 2.4 and 1.6 respectively; Moroccans, 6.2 and 4.5; Tunisians 6.2 and 4.0[49].

Immigrant families even seem to be sensitive to the differences between one host country and another. This is evident from figure 4.6 overleaf which follows the fertility rates of the Turkish communities in three European countries[50]. As you can see, the rates drop

Matching families

Immigrants typically have larger families than the average in the receiving countries but gradually they adjust their fertility levels downwards to match local norms. And just as Swedish women have more children than German women, so Turkish women have more children in Sweden than in Germany. ■

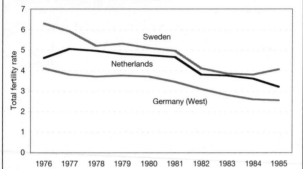

Figure 4.6 – The fertility rates of Turkish women in three host countries, 1976-85

steadily in all three countries. But they are higher in Sweden and the Netherlands than in Germany – probably because the fertility rates of Swedish and Dutch women are higher than those of German women.

So is immigration an answer to shrinking populations in richer countries? If the aim is simply to sustain overall numbers, yes it is. But if the aim is to rejuvenate the population and to ensure that there are enough workers to support elderly people then immigration is not an easy option. In theory you could keep up the number of workers by only allowing in young immigrants, work them hard until they started to show a few gray hairs, and then show them the door. Even if that were desirable, in practice few countries can control temporary migration so precisely. Immigrants have the same rights to a social and family life as anyone, and many immigrants will stay, will be joined by their families, and will have more children. Attempts to force immigrants out en masse usually prove futile. Most countries eventually declare amnesties – 'regularizations' of those who have entered illegally or have overstayed their visas. Anything more forceful usually draws protests from the more liberal section of the host population. A country like Singapore, which has the advantage of being compact and easy to police, and whose government is not overly sensitive to human rights protestors, can exercise fairly tight control. But elsewhere the opportunities are limited. Governments may try to ensure that immigration is biased towards the young – as do those of Canada and Australia, which give preference to younger applicants – but after that they have little influence on the age structure of the immigrant population.

The United Nations Population Division has made rough estimates for a number of countries and regions of just how many immigrants would be needed over the next 50 years to offset the effects of falling birth rates and ageing. The results are shown in table 4.4. These are based on the world population projections made in 1998, and are the best-guess 'medium variant'. To achieve comparability across the countries the

Table 4.4 – Net annual immigration flows over the period 1995-2050 to achieve population objectives

	Current flows	For constant population	For constant support ratio
France	7,000	109,000	1,792,000
Germany	204,000	487,000	3,630,000
Italy	6,000	372,000	2,268,000
Japan	0	647,000	10,471,000
South Korea	-7,000	129,000	102,563,000
Russian Federation	109,000	715,000	5,068,000
United Kingdom	20,000	125,000	1,194,000
United States	760,000	359,000	11,851,000
European Union	270,000	1,588,000	13,480,000

Notes: The constant level and the constant support ratios being aimed at are the highest each country or region would have attained had there been no immigration after 1995.

UN assumed that the age characteristics of the immigrants for all countries would be the same (those of immigrants to the United States). They also assumed that the fertility patterns of immigrants would be the same as those for the host populations, which over a 50-year period is a reasonable approximation.

The first column shows the current average net inflows in recent years (immigration minus emigration). The second column shows how many immigrants it would take annually to keep the population constant. For some countries, such as the United Kingdom, the number of immigrants required to achieve a constant population is not particularly high, and for the United States it is actually around half the current immigration level. But other countries face a more daunting task: Japan would have to take in 715,000 people a year.

The third column shows how many immigrants would be needed each year to maintain a constant support ratio. These are seriously large numbers. The UK would need to absorb over a million people each year which, over this 55-year period, would eventually double the population. But the speculative nature of these calculations is most evident for the South Korea which would need to take in around 100 million people per year. On that reckoning by 2050 Korea would have a population of 7 billion – more than the current population of the whole world.

So you can see that while immigration will clearly help to put a brake on population ageing, in most cases it will be unable to offset it completely. In the end these countries will have to adopt a mixture of policies – increasing fertility rates, raising the retirement age, increasing taxes, and admitting more immigrants.

Objections to immigration

Despite the fact that immigration has had a beneficial impact it almost always generates strong objections. Even in the United States there have always been people who want to shut the doors. Protestors typically argue that although immigration was a good thing in the past, modern immigrants are of such a low quality that it is time to call a halt. A hundred years ago, Francis Walker, then the President of the Massachusetts Institute of Technology, and Superintendent of the US censuses of 1880 and 1890, argued vehemently against further immigration from Europe: 'The entrance into our political, social and industrial life of such vast masses of peasantry is a matter which no intelligent patriot can look upon without the greatest apprehension and alarm…. They are beaten men from beaten races, representing the worst failures in the struggle for existence.'[51] It was this kind of view that led to restrictions on immigration to the United States between the two World Wars.

Such views if expressed more moderately have surfaced throughout America's history. In the mid-1990s they were crystallized in the book, *Alien Nation*. This bemoaned not just the number of aliens arriving, but also that America was becoming a 'freak among the world's nations', and that Americans would become aliens to each other[52]. The author was Peter Brimelow, a British-born immigrant, by then an American citizen, who thought it was time to pull up the drawbridge.

There are also more thoughtful objections. George Borjas, for example, a professor of public policy at Harvard, argues that the United States needs to restrict the number of unskilled immigrants on the grounds that these do not contribute enough to the American economy. Borjas too is an immigrant, from Cuba[53]. Such objections of course take a strictly national perspective, they do not take into account the welfare of the whole population – that is, they exclude the interests of immigrants.

Other countries have also had many people arguing against immigration, usually politicians of the far right trying to stir up racist sentiments. There is a long and dishonorable tradition here, from British politician Enoch Powell's prophecy in 1968 that immigration would lead to 'rivers of blood', to the neo-fascist politics of Austria's Freedom Party, to the One Nation party in Australia. All have been able to tap popular sentiment that prefers to project all problems onto a group of outsiders. Immigrants who look speak and act differently from the rest of the population offer a ready target.

Public opinion polls have regularly reflected popular nervousness about immigration. This is indicated in table 4.5 which collates the results of opinion polls on immigration from four countries on the question

Table 4.5 – Percentage of people wanting to see a decrease in immigration

	United States	Canada	Australia	United Kingdom
1946	37			
1953	39			
1965	33			
1975		39		
1977	42			
1980		42		
1981	65			
1982	66	55		
1983				54
1984				59
1985		42		
1986	49			54
1987		41		
1988	53	41	67	
1989		34	65	53
1990	48	32	64	
1991		45	68	
1992	54	46		
1993	61	45		
Average	50	42	66	55

Simon and Lynch (1999)

of whether immigration should be reduced[54]. Since the polls are not identical in each country, or necessarily comparable from one year to another, the figures can only give a general indication. In the United States there has obviously been some variation over time. But one constant theme in the polls is the 'drawbridge' effect: people think previous immigration was valuable, but that current immigration is not. The 1993 poll, for example, showed that 59 per cent thought that immigration had been good in the past, while 31 per cent thought it had been a bad thing. But when it came to contemporary immigration the figures were reversed.

Canadians on average have been slightly less worried about immigration than US citizens. However the British and also the Australians have been more hostile. In all these countries the respondents consistently favored immigration from each other's countries, or from Europe, compared with the rest of the world. People often express their objections to immigration in economic terms, but in practice most popular objections to immigration are racially motivated. This has been confirmed, for example, by an analysis of the British Social Attitudes Survey over the period 1983-91[55].

For the receiving countries therefore, immigration serves many valuable functions – providing a ready source of labor, and helping to offset declining populations – even if the receiving population is not convinced of the benefits. But what effect does this migration have on the countries the immigrants leave behind?

1 Glover, S., C. Gott, A. Loizillon, Portes, R. Price, S. Spencer, V. Srinivasan and C. Willis (2001). *Migration: An Economic and Social Analysis.* RDS Occasional Paper No 67. London. Home Office.
2 World Bank (2000). *World Development Report*, Washington DC.
3 Freedberg, L. (2000). 'Borderline hypocrisy: do we want them here or not?', in *Washington Post*, February 6. **4** INS (2001). www.ins.usdoj.gov/graphics/services/employerinfo/h1b.htm **5** DeVoretz, D and S. Laryea (1998). *Canadian Human Capital Transfers: The United States and Beyond*, C.D. Howe Institute Commentary 115.

The economic benefits of immigration

www.cdhowe.org **6** New York Times (2000). 'Germany's Immigration Debate', in New York Times, August 12. **7** Economist (2001). 'Bridging Europe's skills gap', in *Economist*, March 31 **8** SOPEMI (2000). *Trends in International Migration*, Paris. OECD. p. 268. **9** DFEE (2000). *Work Permit System will Make it Easier for Firms*. DFEE press release. www.dfee.gov.uk. **10** Economist (2001). 'Bridging Europe's skills gap', in *Economist*, March 31 **11** Migration Dialogue (1999). *Immigration and Integration: Focus on Lyon, France*. http://migration.ucdavis.edu/ols/lyon.html **12** Stalker, P. (1994). *The Work of Strangers*, Geneva, ILO. **13** Abella, M. and Park Y.-b. (1994). 'Labor shortages and foreign workers in small firms of the Republic of Korea' in *Adjustments to Labor shortages and Foreign Workers in the Republic of Korea*, International Migration Papers, No. 1. Geneva, ILO. **14** Werna E. (1997). *Labor Migration in the Construction industry in Latin America and the Caribbean*. Sectoral Activities Programme Working Paper. Geneva, ILO. **15** Garcia, Victor Q. (1997). *Mexican Enclaves in the U.S. Northeast: Immigrant and Migrant Mushroom Workers in Southern Chester County, Pennsylvania*. Indiana University of Pennsylvania Research Report No. 27. **16** Mehrländer, U. (1994). 'The development of post-war migration and refugee policy', in *Immigration as an Economic Asset*, Institute for Public Policy Research, London. **17** Economic Council of Canada. (1991). *New Faces in the Crowd: Economic and social impacts of immigration*, Ottawa. **18** Citizenship and Emigration Canada (1999). *Facts and figures 1999*, Ottawa. **19** Yang, Y. and Zhong, C. (1996). *China's Textile and Clothing Exports in a Changing World Economy*, Economics Division Working Papers, East Asia 96/1, Australian National University, Canberra. **20** Migration News Vol. 8, No. 1, January, 2001. **21** Schmitt, E. (1998). 'Crying Need; Day-Care Quandary: A Nation at War With Itself', in the *New York Times*, January 11. **22** Migration News (2001). Vol. 8, No. 3, March. **23** Travis, A. (2000). 'Cutting off our nose to spite a race', in *The Guardian*, February 17. **24** SOPEMI (1997). *Trends in International Migration*, Paris, OECD. **25** Tapinos, G. (1994). 'The macroeconomic impact of immigration: Review of the literature published since the mid-1970s', in *Trends in International Migration*, Paris, SOPEMI/OECD. **26** Fix, M. and Passel, J. (1994). *Immigration and Immigrants: Setting the Record Straight*. Washington DC, Urban Institute. **27** Butcher, K. and Card, D. (1991). 'Immigration and wages: Evidence from the 1980s', in *American Economic Review*, Vol. 81, No. 2. **28** US Commission on Immigration Reform (1997). *Becoming an American: Immigration and Immigrant Policy*. **29** Castles, S. Iredale, R., and Vasta, E. (1994). 'Australian immigration between globalization and recession', in *International Migration Review*, Vol. 28, No. 2. **30** Econtech (2001). *The Economic Impact of 2000/01 Migration programme Changes*. Report prepared for the Department of Immigration and Multicultural Affairs. **31** Economic Council of Canada. (1991). *New Faces in the Crowd: Economic and Social Impacts of Immigration*. Ottawa. **32** Roy, A. (1997). 'Job displacement effects of Canadian immigrants by country of origin and occupation', in *International Migration Review*, Vol. 31, No. 1. **33** Borjas, G. (1994). 'The economics of immigration', in *Journal* *of Economic Literature*, Vol. 32 **34** Findlay, A. (1994). 'An economic audit of contemporary immigration', in S. Spencer (ed.) *Strangers & Citizens: A Positive Approach to Migrants and Refugees*. London, Institute for Public Policy Research. **35** Zimmerman, K. (1994). 'The labour market impact of immigration', in *Immigration as an Economic Asset*, London, Institute for Public Policy Research. **36** Glover et al (2001). p. 37. **37** Carrington, W. and De Lima, P. (1996). 'The impact of 1970s repatriates from Africa on the Portuguese labor market', in *Industrial and Labor Relations Review*, Vol. 49, No. 2. **38** Glover et al (2001). p. 32. **39** Carnegie Endowment (1996). 'Immigrants and Welfare', in *Research Perspectives on Migration*, Vol.1 No. 1. **40** Fix. M. and Passel J. (1999). *Trends in Non-citizens' and Citizens' use of Public Benefits following Welfare Reform: 1994–97*. Urban Institute, Washington DC. **41** Simon, J. (1989) *The Economic Consequences of Immigration*, Oxford, Blackwell. **42** Smith J. and Edmonston B. (1997). *The New Americans: Economic Demographic and Fiscal Effects of Immigration*. National Academy Press. Available online at: http://stills.nap.edu/books/0309063566/html/ **43** Glover et al (2001). p. 44 **44** United Nations Population Division (2000). Replacement Migration: Is it a Solution to Declining and Ageing Population?, New York, United Nations. **45** United Nations Population Division (2000). *Replacement Migration: Is it a Solution to Declining and Ageing Population?*, United Nations, New York. **46** UN Population Division (2000). *World population prospects: the 2000 Revision*, United Nations, New York. **47** United Nations Population Division (2000). *Replacement Migration: Is it a Solution to Declining and Ageing Population?*, New York, United Nations. Chapter 5, p. 1 **48** World Bank (2000). *World Development Report*, Washington DC. **49** SOPEMI (1989). **50** Stalker, P. (1994). **51** Weiner, M. (1990). 'Immigration: perspectives from receiving countries', in *Third World Quarterly*, Vol. 12, No. 1. **52** Brimelow, P. (1995). *Alien nation: Common Sense about America's Immigration Disaster*. New York, Random House. **53** Borjas, G. (1999). *Heaven's Door: Immigration Policy and the American Economy*, Princeton University Press. **54** Simon, R and J. Lynch (1999). 'A comparative assessment of public opinion towards immigrants and immigration policy', in *International Migration Review*, Vol. 33, No. 2. **55** Dustman, C. and I. Preston (2000). *Racial and Economic Factors in Attitudes to Immigration*, London, Centre for Economic Policy Research, Discussion Paper No. 2542.

5 Emigrants as heroes

If the receiving countries benefit from international migration do the sending countries lose out? Not necessarily. Although developing countries do donate many skilled and educated people to the industrial countries, they also gain more than $60 billion each year in remittances. Nor do they always lose people completely. Nowadays the world is moving more towards the creation of 'transnational communities'.

International migrants are often the healthier, more enterprising people – the very citizens that poor countries can least afford to lose. You might conclude therefore that mass emigration from any developing country would be a national disaster. But governments of the sending countries do not see it that way – and treat emigrants not as traitors but as heroes. Every year at Christmas the government of the Philippines prepares a special welcome for the 100,000 or so Filipinos who are coming home for the holidays. In 2000, this included a 'welcome station' at the Ninoy Aquino International Airport in Manila, and a handout of prizes for many lucky workers. Why all the excitement? The reason is financial. The government of the Philippines is profoundly grateful for the $7 billion that migrants send home each year in remittances. The government of Mexico has also started referring to its citizens working in the US as 'heroes' or 'VIPs', in gratitude for a very similar sum – $6 to $7 billion a year.

In principle, international migration should produce benefits for both receiving and sending countries. This after all is a form of trade, and fair trade allows all parties to gain. But not all international trade is fair, and in international migration too there are winners and losers.

Relieving population pressure

For the sending countries, one possible benefit of international migration would be to relieve population pressure and reduce unemployment. Most have no shortage of people: over the next 50 years the population of the less developed regions as a whole is expected to rise from 4.9 billion to 8.2 billion[1]. And many countries have in the past sent a significant proportion of their population overseas. Between 1846 and 1924, the British Isles (what is now the UK plus Ireland) sent 16 million people to North America and Australia, equivalent to 41 per cent of the 1910 population[2].

Nowadays the proportions leaving developing countries tend to be smaller. True, some of the smallest countries have been effectively depopulated by emigration: over half of people born in the Cook Islands, for example, now live in Aotearoa/New Zealand. But for the major sending countries, even those with the largest numbers of people overseas, a far smaller fraction of the population is leaving. The largest transfer is from Mexico to the United States. Of the 108 million people alive today who were born in Mexico around 8 million now live in the United States – and around 300,000 more Mexicans emigrate each year. This has the effect of reducing Mexico's annual population growth rate from 1.8 per cent to 1.5 per cent[3]. The other major exporter, the Philippines, has around 5 million people overseas which is equivalent to 6 per cent of the population. Globally, however, the demographic impact of emigration is far smaller. The world's population is growing by 77 million annually, but only two to three million people migrate each year.

Because relatively few people leave, emigration cannot usually have much impact on unemployment. Not that there is much 'unemployment' anyway. Most workers in developing countries do not get unemployment benefit if they lose their job, so they must do some kind of work to survive, no matter how unproductive or low paid. In Bangladesh, for example, official unemployment is usually around 2 per cent. But a further 20 per cent of people are officially 'underemployed', in that they are working less than 35 hours per week, while many more are doing low-paid work in the 'informal sector' as street vendors, say, or garbage pickers. At least 40 million Bangladeshis are therefore underemployed. Meanwhile only around 2 million are working overseas[4].

In any case, emigration would not necessarily relieve unemployment or underemployment directly. It costs money to go travel, so those best placed to move are those with some kind of work already and who have savings that can be used to invest in an overseas trip, or at least have collateral against which they can borrow. Nevertheless their departure should open up opportunities for others to step into the jobs they vacate.

Employment problems in developing countries are not going to be solved by emigration. Just as in the receiving countries, the balance between the number of jobs and the number of workers depends more on the efficiency of the economy in creating the right kind of opportunities. This in turn depends on a host of factors, particularly on the health and education of the workforce. The total number of people is only part of the equation. If all the emigrants suddenly returned home there would be a noticeable impact, as happened for example after the Gulf War when around 2 million people were driven out of Kuwait and Iraq, and tried to find work at home. Even then, most of those people were soon reabsorbed into the local workforces. In the longer term the critical issue is not the overall number of workers but the type of people who are leaving or arriving.

The brain drain

One of the main dangers for sending countries is that they might be losing some of the people who have had the most invested in them. Sending unskilled laborers is one thing, but sending highly trained professionals is another. If a country has spent thousands of dollars educating a doctor or an engineer, it can lose years of investment in a matter of hours when that person gets on a plane to take their skills elsewhere.*

It is difficult to estimate the extent of the brain drain at a global level. This is because the sending countries do not collect information on the educational qualifications of emigrants. And although some of the receiving countries do record such information, they do not do so in a consistent fashion so it is difficult to collate the data. As with so many other aspects of migration, the most comprehensive picture is available for the United States: between 1994 and 1999, the United States imported more than 300,000 people with higher education degrees – including 124,000 Indians, 68,000 Chinese, 57,000 Filipinos, 49,000 Canadians and 42,000 British[5].

However from the sending country's point of view the more significant statistic is not the absolute number of trained people they are losing but the proportion. An IMF study, using the 1990 US Census, made some rough estimates and found that the larger sending countries are losing only a small percentage of their professionals to the United States – India and China had by then lost 1 per cent, and the Philippines and South Korea around 6 per cent[6]. But for other countries the numbers are more worrying. Around 13 per cent of Mexicans with tertiary education now live in the US and for most of Central America the proportion is 15 to 20 per cent.

For Caribbean countries, the situation is even more alarming – around 60 per cent of people who received tertiary education in Jamaica or in Trinidad and Tobago were living in the US. Guyana in South America lost 70 per cent of its college graduates. Within Asia the highest losses were for Iran (15 per cent) and Taiwan (8 per cent); and within Africa,

Gambia (60 per cent) and Sierra Leone (25 per cent).

But migration to the United States is only a part of the problem, since professionals also head for Europe, Australia and elsewhere. This is less easy to assess since few other countries collect the information so systematically. Nevertheless, it should be possible to extrapolate from the US experience – assuming, for example, that immigrants to Europe are educationally equivalent to those going to the United States. This will not be true for some sending countries: most people who go from Africa to the US, for example, are professionals, while most Africans going to Europe are unskilled. Nevertheless, if one chooses the countries where the assumptions seem plausible it is possible to make a more realistic estimation. For Asian countries, the IMF estimates that the proportion of professionals they are losing to the industrial countries as a whole are: Iran 25 per cent, South Korea, 15 per cent; the Philippines 10 per cent; India 3 per cent; and China 3 per cent.

Of the African countries for which reliable estimates are possible, one of the highest proportions is for Ghana at 26 per cent. For South Africa and Egypt the proportion is around 8 per cent. In the Caribbean, one of the most dramatic exoduses has been from Jamaica: some 77 per cent of Jamaicans with tertiary education live outside the country; indeed one-third of Jamaicans with secondary education now live overseas[7].

The proportions are far higher for emigrants working in research and development. In 1999 a study prepared for UNESCO estimated that there were at least 400,000 scientists and engineers from developing countries working in research and development in the industrial countries – compared with around 1.4 million still working at home[8].

Not all professional migration is from poor countries to rich. There is also a constant circulation of people between the industrial countries. Canada has a large import-export trade in professionals. In 1996, when 11,000 Canadian professionals left for the US, 18,000 immigrant professionals arrived from else-where[9]. There is also a constant swirl of educated people moving around Asia, as well as between Asia and the countries of the Gulf. And following the collapse of communism, there has also been a rapid flow of professionals from Eastern Europe to Western Europe and the United States.

You can understand why professionals would want to move. In South Africa, for example, primary school teachers and nurses in 2000 were earning only $450 per month and hundreds were leaving each month for better-paid jobs in the UK, Australia and Saudi Arabia. But money is not the only consideration. Professionals also want to pursue their careers. And if they are also worried about the prospects for political or economic stability they are even more likely to emigrate. Since the end of apartheid there has been a large exodus from South Africa, which is thought to have lost over one million skilled workers, managers and other professionals. Difficult conditions in the Soviet Union and Iran have also caused many thousands of people to leave. The temptation is even greater for people working in science and technology, who will not only get paid more overseas but will also be to use the facilities of well-funded university and corporate laboratories. A survey in Bangladesh in 2000 found that 72 per cent of information technology specialists and 85 per cent of information technology students planned to emigrate to take advantage of better opportunities abroad[10].

The brain drain is also a direct consequence of the immigration policies of the richer countries, all of whom go out of their way to attract skilled immigrants. Australia and Canada have well-organized systems that make it easier for highly-qualified people to enter. The United States has also been increasing the number of visas available for skilled workers. Even the United Kingdom, which has closed the door to most forms of immigration, is now making it easier for employers to draw in skilled workers from overseas.

A more indirect way of acquiring professionals is to enroll foreign students. Universities and colleges in many countries see foreign students as a rich source of income and run aggressive marketing programs, particularly in Asia where they often have partnerships with local institutions. Since most students want to learn English, the English-speaking countries have an advantage. The largest number of foreign students are in the United States – 560,000[11]. Next comes the United Kingdom which in 1998 had 266,000, and pocketed around $600 million in fees. In 2000 the British government said it intended to increase its share of the English-speaking higher education market – from 17 to 25 per cent – with a $7-million marketing campaign. The French government has also gone on the offensive, determined as ever to promote French language and culture and in 1998 it announced a $17-million program to attract foreign students who in that year accounted for 130,000 of France's two million college students. Many of these people, particularly those studying for advanced degrees, will not return home. In the US only half of the foreign students receiving a doctorate or a post-doctoral qualification return to their native country within two years[12]. According to UNESCO, as many as 30,000 Africans holding PhD degrees are now living outside the continent[13].

How damaging is this brain drain for the sending countries? There are a number of costs. One is that those who leave are often the best and the brightest – so their departure reduces the country's capacity for long-term economic growth and human development. A second is that it deprives the country of many urgently needed skills. This is most evident in medicine. The industrial countries seem to have an insatiable appetite for doctors and nurses, many from developing countries. Over the period 1978-85,

Jamaica lost around 80 per cent of the doctors it had trained, leaving it with a severe shortage of medical staff[14]. The situation is equally severe in many African countries: Ghana, for example, lost 60 per cent of the doctors it trained in the early 1980s[15].

Added to this is the financial cost. A simple calculation will show a rough order of magnitude. For the OECD countries as a whole there are around three million immigrants with a tertiary education. If it costs say $20,000 to educate someone to this level, then the total wealth transferred from poor countries to rich is now around $60 billion.

Nevertheless, the flows of skilled people should not be seen simply as a loss. Many developing countries have more graduates than they need. Responding to the aspirations of the middle and upper classes, governments often overspend on tertiary education. India, for example, regularly produces more science graduates than it can employ. A number of African countries also have surplus graduates in certain subjects. In these circumstances it makes sense to send them overseas where they can recoup some of the cost of their education. There are also many cases where people are paying for their own education or training specifically to qualify for overseas employment. Private medical schools in the Philippines, for example, advertise for students, guaranteeing them a job in the United States once they graduate. This phenomenon has now spread to information technology. India is awash with computer training institutions, where tuition costs between $4 to $100 a month[16].

Sending the money home – flows of remittances

One reason why it might make sense to train people to work overseas is that they send much of their income back in the form of remittances. If the migrants are traveling for temporary work, they usually live frugally to save as much as possible, either to take back when they return or to send to the family at home. An undocumented Mexican worker in the United States, for example, might be sending back $500 per month, and the Philippines Central Bank believes that the country's five million overseas workers on average send back over $400 per month. It used to be thought that these remittances would decline as migrants put down roots in their new countries, but this does not seem to be the case, and remittances to developing countries and Eastern Europe have continued to grow steadily, reaching over $65 billion by 1999 (figure 5.1). However, this is not a net inflow into developing countries since many of these remittances pass from one developing country to another. Thus, while Malaysia gains $300 million from Malaysians abroad, it loses $2.4 billion to other countries.

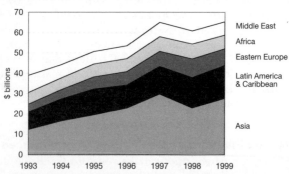

Cashback

Immigrants from developing countries and Eastern Europe send home around $65 billion in remittances each year. But this is just the money that travels through official banking channels. Taking into account the funds carried or transmitted unofficially, the annual total is probably well above $100 billion. ■

Figure 5.1 – Remittances to developing countries and Eastern Europe, 1993-99

Notes: Turkey is included within Eastern Europe.

IMF (2000).

But this refers only to official transfers. Studies in individual developing countries suggest that migrants on average send only around half of remittances through official banking channels. This is because they are discouraged by high fees and poor rates of exchange: if they want to send $300 from the United States to Mexico via either of the two main companies, Western Union or Moneygram, for example, they have to pay around $30. Some migrants therefore just carry back a bag of cash, or cart home expensive consumer goods, or send money with friends. Others use professional money couriers – the *padala* system in the Philippines, for example, or the *hundi* system in the Indian subcontinent. These take foreign currency from the emigrants and hand over local currency to the family back home. In southern Africa, migrants send money through an informal network of taxi and bus drivers. Allowing for the funds that pass through unofficial channels, the global flow of remittances to developing countries is probably more than $100 billion.

For some countries, remittances have become a vital source of income and foreign exchange. In Egypt, for example, remittances from migrants have at times generated as much foreign exchange as tourism, oil exports, and the income from the Suez Canal combined. Table 5.1 overleaf shows the top 20 receiving countries, and the proportion that remittances represent of their total economies – their gross domestic products (GDPs). Some of the smaller countries in particular are very dependent on remittances. For Yemen, remittances are equivalent to 25 per cent of GDP.

The dependence on remittances is even greater for individual communities. In Lesotho, for example, more than 40 per cent of householders have reported that their principle sources of income are remittances from South Africa. In the Philippines around 15 per cent of households receive income from abroad[17].

Emigrants as heroes

When emigrants start sending money back, their families may suddenly find they have an income two or three times greater than before, and sometimes far more. What do they do with it? Many, particularly in Africa, will immediately spend more on food and other household essentials. In the land around the Senegal river in Mali, for example, families depend heavily on remittances from relatives in France to meet food deficits[18]. After meeting immediate needs

Table 5.1 – Top 20 developing country receivers of remittances, 1999

Rank	Country	$ millions	percentage of GDP
1.	India	11,097	2.6
2.	Philippines	7,016	8.9
3.	Mexico	6,649	1.7
4.	Turkey	4,529	2.3
5.	Egypt	3,196	4.0
6.	Morocco	1,918	5.5
7.	Bangladesh	1,803	4.1
8.	Pakistan*	1,707	2.7
9.	Dominican Rep	1,613	11.0
10.	Thailand	1,460	1.1
11.	Jordan	1,460	21.2
12.	El Salvador	1,379	12.3
13.	Nigeria	1,292	3.5
14.	Yemen*	1,202	24.5
15.	Brazil	1,192	0.2
16.	Indonesia	1,109	0.8
17.	Ecuador	1,084	5.8
18.	Sri Lanka	1,056	6.9
19.	Tunisia	761	4.0
20.	Peru	712	1.2

Note: These data combine two IMF categories: 'compensation of employees', and 'workers remittances', which correspond to flows from short-term and longer-term migrants, respectively – subtracting debits from credits to give net remittances. The GNP figure used for the second column is for 1998. *For Pakistan the data are for 1997, and for Yemen 1998.

IMF (2000), World Bank (2000)

for food and clothing and children's education, the migrants' families typically invest in housing. Migrants' houses frequently stand out in the neighborhood. In Ecuador, for example, the provinces of Azuay and Canar are noted for their 'migrant mansions'. And in Fujian province in China, many large homes are now springing up – frequently owned by 'widows' whose husbands are working illegally in the United States. The families of emigrants also commonly buy land. While some may do so in order to extend their own farms, they can also treat land as a form of saving or investment. This may benefit the families concerned, but it also reduces the land available for others: in the Caribbean many returning migrants have bought land speculatively and driven up prices. Although families of migrants do splash out on consumer goods, housing and land, they also save. In the Philippines families with remittances save a higher proportion of their income than the rest of the population[19].

Another possibility is to invest in new businesses. There is no reason why migrants or their families should be any more entrepreneurial than the rest of the population, particularly if the emigrants have had little education. And many come from poor communities that do not offer many opportunities for investment. Nevertheless current or former migrants do invest in enterprises that require only small amounts of capital, such as stores, restaurants or workshops. In the Dominican Republic, for example, migrants have established small factories, and many other kinds of commercial establishment. One study of such firms in the late 1980s found that they had been started on average with around $12,000 but continued to receive fresh injections of capital from migrants in the United States[20].

Migrant remittances also have a beneficial 'multiplier effect' on the economy as a whole. For Mexico, the $2 billion in 'migradollars' that were arriving in the early 1990s are thought to have increased overall annual production by $6.5 billion. This was because agricultural communities, for example, used remittances to buy more equipment, fertilizers and other items that helped to increase output[21]. But even when people use remittances to pay for food say, or health care, or to enable children to stay at school, this promotes human development and boosts long-term productivity, helping to make the country as a whole wealthier.

Cultures of emigration

Migration might bring financial benefits to the sending communities but it also has social costs. In some countries the majority of migrants have been young men, many of whom are married, placing extra burdens on the shoulders of women who have to maintain the household. The most dramatic effects of male emigration are to be seen in Africa. In Lesotho, where men can leave for up to 15 years to work in South Africa, around half of all married women have spent considerable periods without their husbands, which means they have to work on the farm, trying to sustain the family with remittances that are often inadequate. In many South Asian countries, on the other hand, emigration can bring the extended family into play. In some cases the wife may then stay with other family members, or at least get more frequent visits from parents and in-laws. Often the extended family itself will have organized the emigration, helping to finance the trip, so when the remittances come back from one or more emigrants the whole family pools the funds.

The status of women can thus alter in many possible ways following the emigration of partners. When the woman becomes the head of the family, along with the extra workload she gains greater independence. But when she is absorbed more into the extended family, she may actually be less free. One village study in Pakistan, for example, concluded that greater control by in-laws constrained women's lives far more and strengthened the observation of *purdah*[22].

Nowadays, however, an increasing proportion of migrants are women – they now account for around 48 per cent of international migrants. Men and women migrate to the richer countries in more or less equal numbers, a result partly of family reunification programs, though contract migrants to other developing countries are more likely to be male. In some cases, however, women make up the majority of contract workers, particularly from Sri Lanka, the Philippines, Thailand and Indonesia. The major receiving countries for these women have been Brunei, Japan, Malaysia, Singapore, Kuwait and Saudi Arabia – mostly for work in domestic service and entertainment, as well as in nursing and teaching[23].

A more general concern for communities that send people overseas is the creation of a culture of emigration. This has long been the case in the Caribbean where a history of slavery and indentured labor has left fractured societies in which emigration is seen as one of the most natural options. Young men who have few opportunities at home have come to regard emigration, even if only temporary, as a rite of passage. A similar phenomenon seems to have emerged in Mexico where a whole generation of young people in many communities now direct their aspirations towards *El Norte*.

Going home again

Although most attention is focused on out-migration a significant proportion of migrants return. Most South Asians who spend time as contract workers in the Gulf, for example, go back after a few years. And few Thai men working on collective farms in Israel, or Indonesian women working as domestic servants in Hong Kong, plan to stay very long. For other migrants the situation may be more ambiguous – many spend their lives haunted by the 'myth of return'. Many

South Asians who arrived in the UK during the 1960s and 1970s seriously intended to return home eventually, but never did. And of the 'guest workers' who came to Germany in the 1970s up to one-third are thought to have remained.

On the other hand, many people who migrate with the aim of long-term settlement change their minds after a couple of years. Of the 30 million people admitted to the US between 1900 and 1980 10 million are believed to have returned[24]. Another study has concluded that around 20 per cent leave the United States within ten years of arrival and one-third leave over their lifetime[25].

Some return out of disappointment. Others leave when they have accumulated sufficient funds. But often the deciding factor will be the situation in the home country. If the economic outlook improves then returning will seem a more attractive proposition. Ireland, for example, has long been a country of emigration – more than one million Irish people live abroad (around 40 million people in the US claim Irish ancestry). But Ireland's economic boom is encouraging many to return. By the middle of 1999 Ireland was receiving over 1,000 immigrants per week, of whom more than half were returning Irish[26].

Many people have also been going back to Asia to take advantage of new opportunities. Indeed Asian governments that find themselves short of skilled labor have been going out of their way to woo their expatriates. In Taiwan, where many people are returning to work in high-tech industries, this is called *rencai huiliu* – the 'return flow of human talent'. There are also many opportunities in both Taiwan and China for people to work in US transnationals. Many Chinese who had gone to the US as students and stayed on to work and become naturalized citizens are now much sought after in Asia. US companies also like to employ 'ABCs' (American-born Chinese), the children of immigrants, who usually also speak some Chinese.

The return home will not always be smooth. Returning migrants, who are often wealthier than the people around them can stir resentment. Thus West Indian migrants who have spent most of their lives in the UK and return home to retire can find themselves a ready target for crime. Some returning migrants who find it difficult to settle will remigrate. One estimate suggests that 15 per cent of those who return to Barbados are so disappointed that they migrate again back to the UK or North America. There can also be cultural clashes. Japanese settlers or their descendants returning from Brazil may look physically identical to other Japanese, but they act, and even move, very differently – after a period in Brazil they are far more flamboyant.

Transnational communities

For many migrants, however, life is more complex as they move back and forth from their home country to their host country. This kind of circular migration is very common between Mexico and the United States. Although migrants prefer the wages in the United States they find life more amenable in Mexico and try to get the best of both worlds. International migration is thus generating a new kind of social space, occupied by 'transnational communities'. Overseas diasporas are nothing new: Jews, Armenians, and many others have maintained scattered communities all over the world. But nowadays, with cheaper transport and communications, it is easier for people abroad to maintain far closer links with their home village or neighborhood.

International telecommunications traffic has increased dramatically, driven largely by the voice and data demands of international business. But international migrants have been able to take full advantage of this to keep in close touch with their home communities. The telecommunications companies have not been slow to spot the market opportunity: companies in the United States, for example, run special promotions to coincide with the national holidays of different ethnic groups.

And in the emigrants' countries the telephone has taken on a new significance. In many towns in El Salvador, for example, the main locus of social activity is no longer the church or the plaza but the office of the local telephone company, Antel. In one town of 3,000 people, the operator places around 400 collect calls per month to the United States. The Mexican telephone company, Telmex, has made things even easier by opening branches in California that will allow migrants to pay the telephone bills of their families back home. Newer forms of communication have increased the options for transnational links: immigrants in the US and elsewhere can go into public libraries and use the internet to read the newspapers in their home communities as well as communicate via email and chat rooms.

The possibilities for calling home have increased dramatically with the availability of mobile telephones, which in the rural areas of many developing countries have overnight put some of the remotest places in touch with the outside world. Bangladesh's Grameen Bank, for example, the pioneer of micro-credit for rural women, has launched Grameen Telecom which offers village women another income-earning opportunity. Now the women can sell mobile telephone time via a 'Village Phone' to their neighbors – allowing families to keep in close contact with sons and daughters in the Gulf or in Southeast Asia. While most of the outgoing calls are local, the majority of incoming calls are international. One useful function here is to enable families to monitor the flow of remittances. Many Bangladeshi migrants avoid the official banking system which offers them a bad rate of exchange. They prefer to use couriers – often other migrants who are returning home. This is a risky business and the money is often lost or delayed, but the Village Phone enables people to monitor this activity much more closely[27].

Although most remittances stay within families, there are also many examples of migrants supporting community development back home. Mexicans in the United States, for example, have around 1,500 'hometown associations', which have supported all kinds of community activity, from building new roads to repainting the church to paying for fiestas. Similarly, emigrants from El Salvador who live in Los Angeles, Washington DC and many other US cities have established *comités del pueblo* (town committees) to support activities back home. Salvadoran towns with this kind of association often acquire paved roads and electricity – as well as fancier strips for the local football team[28].

These associations are also investing in businesses. The Mexican state of Jalisco, for example, now has an 'Economic Development Fund'. The 50 or so Jalisco hometown associations in Los Angeles invest in this and the Mexican government provides matching funds. A Mexico City-based money transfer company, Raza Express, also contributes 75¢ for each $300 remitted to Mexico. In the town of Etzatlán, for example, this has been used to invest in clothing and furniture factories to create many new jobs[29]. Similarly in the state of Guanajuanto, 80 US-based migrants have invested $10 million in factories in their areas of origin, including several sewing factories employing 600 people in Ocampo[30].

Links have also been established between Europe and Africa. Many of the Malian immigrants to France come from the Kayes region. Some 70 per cent of these are active members of their village associations. A study in 1996 found that over ten years these migrants had contributed more than $2 million to finance 146 projects, a sum supplemented with around $0.5 million from non-governmental organizations. Migrant funds are thought to have contributed to more than half the region's infrastructure[31].

Migrants, including refugees, also send relief funds to people at home. Minnesota, for example, now has around 50,000 Somali refugees. They work hard, often holding multiple jobs – as night watchmen, parking-lot attendants, taxi drivers, coffee shop operators and restaurateurs – and many are devout Muslims who feel a strong obligation to help their home communities. According to a Minneapolis-based money-transfer firm, Somali Global Service, one Somali in the United States can support more than 10 people in the refugee camps. Some are sending up to 75 per cent of their incomes to relatives in Kenya and elsewhere. The local Somali-run coffee shops also serve as collection points, gathering small change from customers to channel home via the local mosque.[32]

Jet-setting emigrants

At the other end of the transnational scale are the jet-setting entrepreneurs. Many wealthy Chinese have extensive business interests in Hong Kong, Taiwan, mainland China and elsewhere in Asia, but prefer the security of a passport from Australia, or Canada, or Aotearoa/New Zealand. They therefore emigrate with their families then travel back and forth to work – and are commonly referred to as 'astronauts'. In this case paradoxically it is the family that has emigrated rather than the worker. Prior to the handover of Hong Kong to China, large numbers of these flexible families settled in Vancouver, taking advantage of Canada's business migration program. Children of the astronauts are often termed 'satellite kids'. There is some debate over whether the people in this hypermobile elite constitute a new globalized 'overclass', or have been forced into the astronaut lifestyle because they find it difficult to do business in Canada[33]. Either way, they seem to do quite well out of it financially, even if this puts enormous strain on the family, particularly on the isolated wives (there are very few female astronauts)[34].

For the immigrants themselves international migration is usually a good idea. One study concluded that entering the United States as a legal immigrant was equivalent to winning $10,000, and over a lifetime the gain would be $300,000[35]. But it also seems that the economies of developing countries benefit. Nevertheless most people would not choose to leave home unless they really had to. Will more people do so in future? That is the subject of the final chapter.

1 United Nations (2000). *World Population Prospects: The 2000 Revision*, New York, United Nations. 2 Massey, D. (1988). 'Economic development and international migration in comparative perspective', in *Population and Development Review*, Vol. 14, No. 2, New York. 3 Martin, P. and M. Teitelbaum (2000). *Emigration and Development: Focus on West-central Mexico*. Report of the eighth Migration Dialogue seminar. 4 Stalker, P. (2000). *Workers without Frontiers*, ILO/Lynne Rienner. 5 Garelle, S. (2001). *World Competitiveness Yearbook 2001*. Lausanne, International Institute for Management Development. 6 Carrington, J. and E. Detragiache (1999). 'How extensive is the brain drain?', in *Finance and Development*, Vol. 36, No. 2. 7 Garelle, S. (2001). *World Competitiveness Yearbook 2001*. Lausanne, International Institute for Management Development. 8 Meyer, B. and Brown, M. (1999). *Scientific Diasporas: A new Approach to the Brain Drain*, Management of Social Transformations, Discussion Paper No. 41 Paris, UNESCO. 9 Migration News (1999), Vol. 6, No. 7, July. 10 UNB (2000). '85% of students studying IT want to leave country', Dhaka, United News of Bangladesh. 11 *Migration News* (1998), Vol. 5, No. 12, December 12 Meyer, B. and Brown, M. (1999). *Scientific Diasporas: A new Approach to the Brain Drain*, Management of Social Transformations, Discussion Paper No. 41 Paris, UNESCO 13 Deen, T. (1999). 'Africa's brain drain accelerates', in *Daily Mail and Guardian*, Johannesburg, February 10. 14 Anderson, P. (1988). 'Manpower losses and employment adequacy among skilled workers in Jamaica, 1976-85', in *When Borders don't Divide*, New York, Center for Migration Studies. 15 Stalker, P. (2000). *Workers without Frontiers*, ILO/Lynne Rienner p. 107. 16 *Migration News* (1998), Vol. 5, No. 2, February 17 Stalker, P. (1994). *The Work of Strangers*, Geneva, ILO. p. 126. 18 Hatton, T. and Williamson, J. (2001). *Demographic and Economic Pressures on Immigration out of Africa*, National Bureau of Economic Research, Working Paper 8124, Cambridge, Mass. 19 Stalker, P. (1994). *The Work of Strangers*, Geneva, ILO. 20 Portes, A. (1997). *Globalization from Below: The Rise of Transnational Communities*. Princeton University. 21 Durand, J., Parrado E., and Massey D. (1996). 'Migradollars and development: A reconsideration of the Mexican case', in *International Migration Review*, Vol. 30, No. 2. p. 423 22 Lefebvre, A. (1990).

Emigrants as heroes

'International migration from two Pakistani villages with different forms of agriculture', in *The Pakistan Development Review*, Vol. 29, No. 1.

23 UN Commission on Population and Development (1997). *Concise Report on World Population Monitoring, 1997: International Migration and Development*, New York. United Nations. **24** Shapiro, M. (1992). 'Leaving America', in *World Monitor*, April. **25** Bratsberg, B. and Terrell, D. 1996. 'Where do Americans live abroad?', in *International Migration Review*, Vol. 30, No. 3 **26** Stalker, P. (2000). *Handbook of the World*, Oxford, OUP. **27** Richardson, D. R Ramirez, and Haq, M. (2000). *Grameen Telecom's Village Phone Programme in Rural Bangladesh: A Multimedia Case Study*. Guelph Ontario, TeleCommons Development Group. **28** Portes, A. (1997). Op. cit. **29** Romney, L. (1999). 'Immigrants tapped to fund jobs in Mexico', in *Los Angeles Times*, August 6. **30** Martin, P. and Teitelbaum, M. (2000). Op. cit. **31** Libercier, M. and Schneider, H. (1996). *Migrants: Partners in Development Co-operation*, Paris, OECD. **32** DePass, D and Powell, J. (2000). 'Somali refugees send big share of income back home', *Minnesota Star Tribune*, November 19. **33** Ley. D (2000). *Seeking Homo-economicus: The Strange Story of Canada's Business Immigration Program*. Vancouver, Research on Immigration and Integration in the Metropolis, Working Paper No. 00-002. **34** Waters, J. (2001). *The Flexible Family? Recent Immigration and 'Astronaut' Households in Vancouver, British Columbia*. Research on Immigration and Integration in the Metropolis, Working Paper No, 01-002 **35** Economist (2000). 'Who gains?', in *Economist*, March 9.

6 Shock absorbers for the global economy

Globalization should in principle equalize international incomes, and thus help replace flows of people with flows of goods and finance. In fact however, globalization is so distorted that it is making the world increasingly unequal – shaking even more people loose and encouraging them to undertake dangerous journeys for exploitative work. International migrants have become the shock absorbers for the global economy.

THE CENTRAL PROMISE – or threat – of globalization is that countries all over the world should become increasingly alike. Not just that there will be a branch of McDonalds or the Gap in every shopping mall, but that incomes around the world should eventually converge so that there should be no need to look for work abroad.

How likely is this? Certainly in the past there have been periods of international convergence between the richer countries. One was in the period 1870-1913 when European wages moved closer to those in the United States and Australia. Another was in the 1960s when Europe again caught up with the US and within Europe the incomes of the poorer countries – Portugal, Spain and Italy – moved closer towards those of France and Germany[1]. In Europe this convergence certainly reduced migration: during the period 1966-70, around 250,000 Italians emigrated, but by 1976-80 more people were arriving in Italy than leaving[2].

In most of the rest of the world, however, the picture has been very different – as the richer countries pulled further and further ahead of the developing countries. In 1870 the per capita income of the United States was nine times greater than that of the world's poorest countries, but by 1960 it was 50 times greater[3].

Since then, the experience has been no better. In 1996 the UNDP *Human Development Report* calculated that between 1960 and 1993 the share of global income going to the richest 20 per cent of the world's people rose from 70 to 85 per cent , while that of the poorest 20 per cent fell from 2.3 to 1.4 per cent[4]. Even in the brief period 1988-93, global inequality continued to increase: the share of the world's income going to the richest 10 per cent of the world's population rose from 48 to 52 per cent , while that of the poorest 10 per cent fell from 0.88 to 0.64 per cent[5].

Migration in a globalizing world

This divergence is very different from that predicted by classical economic theory, which says that the movement of capital, goods, and people across national borders should eventually bring prices and wages everywhere into line. Workers should move from low-wage countries to high-wage countries to meet labor shortages. Theoretically this should help balance incomes – restraining them in the rich countries, and boosting them in the poor countries. Meanwhile capital should be moving in the other direction – seeking out places where investment funds are scarcer and the rates of profit higher. The poorer countries should then be able to send goods instead of people. In economic terms this is referred to as 'factor price equalization', the 'factors' in this case being capital and labor. Clearly this is not happening. Neither people, nor goods, nor capital are flowing in the free and beneficial fashion that this simple model predicts.

Trade instead of migration

One of the most obvious benefits of fairer trade between rich and poor countries should be to generate more employment in the migrant-sending countries – and reduce the need for people to go overseas to work. Why have Bangladeshis working in garment sweatshops in New York when they could sit in garment factories in Dhaka and send the shirts instead? Standard trade theory argues that this is what should happen – that trade should substitute for migration. The richer countries, which have more capital, should specialize in the high-tech goods such as cars or machine tools, and the poor countries, which have more workers, should specialize in the labor-intensive ones such as garments or toys. This means that the rich countries have to drop barriers to cheap imports from developing countries, while the developing countries should stop trying to protect inefficient industries that are making goods that could be imported more cheaply from Europe or the US.

In practice things do not work out that way. Trade barriers have fallen but in a lop-sided fashion: the richer countries have forced poor countries to drop their defenses, but have protected their own more vulnerable industries – maintaining import tariffs on precisely those goods such as textiles and garments that developing countries are best placed to export. Meanwhile the poorest countries which are now deep in debt have to submit to the conditions of the International Monetary Fund (IMF) and the World Bank who demand that they open up their economies whether they are ready or not. As a result, globally the tariffs for textiles and clothing are twice as high as the average for industrial goods as a whole[6].

The governments of the 'Asian tiger' economies during the 1970s and 1980s had a more rational approach. They promoted exports but also for a long period maintained import barriers to protect their infant industries. Nowadays the proponents of free trade frown upon such strategies. When in 1987 Mexico joined the forerunner of the World Trade Organization, the General Agreement on Trade and Tariffs, it dropped its average tariff on imports from 45 to 9 per cent. As a result, between 1986 and 1991 imports shot up and in Mexico City alone 500 engineering firms went bankrupt[7].

Even if trade were more genuinely free, however, it is doubtful that it would substitute to any great extent for migration. This is because manufacturing now constitutes a much smaller part of the economies of most industrial countries. Some richer countries do maintain older industries with the help of immigrants. But probably only 10 to 20 per cent of all immigrants in the richer countries work in industries that face direct competition from poorer countries[8].

A more promising form of substitution in the longer term might be through trade in services. Advances in communications and information technology now make it much more feasible to trade services across international borders. Companies in the Caribbean and elsewhere, for example, have been doing more of the simple 'back office' work for global corporations – keying in information, from credit card slips, or airline tickets, so that the data can be fed into computers. Other companies have been transcribing doctors' dictation tapes into medical records. These opportunities will dry up as more sophisticated paperless systems are introduced and as voice-recognition technology improves, but other opportunities are appearing, notably through call centers. India's first international call center, which opened in the mid-1990s, employs more than 5,000 people, whose tasks include chasing up people who have fallen behind on their credit card payments[9]. European or North American consumers dialing up with queries about products or services will find that more and more they could be talking to someone in India or the Philippines. Even so, such work can employ only a tiny, well-educated, proportion of the workforce.

Investment instead of migration

The other means by which globalization might reduce the need for emigration is if financial institutions choose to invest more in developing countries and thus create more employment. In the past, most flows

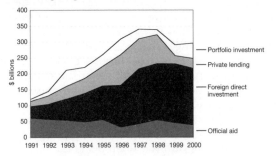

Fluctuating finance

In the early 1990s around half the investment funds going to developing countries arrived as official aid. But nowadays aid is dwarfed by private flows – which may help boost economic growth but can also fluctuate wildly, making people feel less secure and thus fostering emigration. ■

$ billions (y-axis: 0, 50, 100, 150, 200, 250, 300, 350, 400)

x-axis: 1991 1992 1993 1994 1995 1996 1997 1998 1999 2000

— Portfolio investment
— Private lending
— Foreign direct investment
— Official aid

Figure 6.1 – Net flows of finance to developing countries, 1991-2000

UNCTAD (2000)

of capital from rich countries to poor took the form of official aid. In recent years, the picture has changed dramatically: aid has been dwarfed by flows of private investment. This is illustrated in figure 6.1. Between 1990 and 2000 the share of external finance contributed by aid fell from 50 to 13 per cent.

While such investment can create growth and employment it also exposes developing countries to huge risks. This is particularly true of private lending, either through banks or through companies selling bonds to raise cash, because the borrowers have to repay, or pay dividends, in foreign currency. This need not be a problem when the exchange rate is stable. But if there is a drop in the value of the currency then enterprises can soon find themselves unable to service their foreign debts. Another form of capital transfer is portfolio investment. In this case foreign institutions, such as pension funds in the UK, buy shares in companies in Mexico or the Philippines. Again this is fine when the going is good, but if there is an economic crisis foreign investors often take fright as a herd, suddenly selling their shares en masse and triggering a stock market collapse.

The dangers of private lending and portfolio investment were highlighted in 1995 when the Mexican peso suddenly lost about 50 per cent of its value – a result of Mexico accepting huge quantities of foreign funds and using them unwisely. The Mexican economy crashed, throwing thousands of people out of work and cutting the wages of many others. There was a similar scenario in Asia from 1997 when the collapse of the Thai baht sent shock waves around the region. Investors again took fright and sold everything they could. The effects of the Asian financial crisis are evident in figure 6.1, as first portfolio investment and then bank lending suffered steep declines.

A more stable form of capital flow is foreign direct investment – which now accounts for the bulk of finance to developing countries. In this case a transnational company builds or buys a factory and starts producing goods there either for local consumption or export. Since the capital is tied up in physical assets, it is more difficult for the company to leave and so investment is less vulnerable to short-term economic crises. Foreign direct investment could reduce the need for migration in two ways. The first is by directly providing employment. In fact, however, transnationals, whose production is generally very capital-intensive, employ relatively few people directly: in 1999 they had only 40 million people in foreign affiliates all over the world – and more than half of those were in other developed countries[10].

The most labor-intensive production generated by TNCs in developing countries is in export-processing zones (EPZs) – duty-free areas where local people assemble products from imported components to produce finished goods which are then re-exported. One of the highest concentrations of EPZs is along the Mexican-US border in the *maquiladora* (making-up) factories which employ around 1.3 million people, many of them assembling computers and other electronic equipment from components imported from Asia. These factories have a direct connection with cross-border migration. Until 1964 the United States allowed Mexicans to enter legally as seasonal agricultural workers, or *braceros*. When the US government stopped this program the Mexican government encouraged the establishment of the *maquiladoras* to provide alternative employment. However it is doubtful that they served this purpose since the *braceros* were men while the majority of workers in the new factories are women.

The second, longer-term benefit of foreign direct investment in developing countries could be to boost economic growth, not just by providing capital but by transferring technology, training local people, and creating export sales. Here again, however there are grounds for skepticism. Companies generally choose to invest in the places that already have good infrastructure and an educated workforce. As a result investors are more likely to follow growth than to stimulate it. Moreover they also want to invest in countries that offer markets for their output. As a result, most foreign direct investment goes from one developed country to another. In 1999 just 25 per cent of foreign direct investment went to developing countries, and much of that was concentrated in a few favored countries such as China, Mexico, Brazil, and several countries in Southeast Asia[11]. It seems unlikely therefore that either trade or investment will create sufficient employment to absorb the millions of people who enter the workforce each year.

Development disruption

In fact, in the short term, the disruption caused by globalization and industrialization in general are more likely to provoke additional emigration. The industrial revolution in 19th-century Europe forced people to become more mobile and contributed to mass emigration to North America and Australia. Similar processes are at work in most developing countries today, as people move from the countryside to the cities where they have far more disrupted and fragmented lifestyles – and are exposed to many new possibilities, including the option of emigration. They are also more likely to find the funds and contacts that can help them leave. But just as mass emigration from Europe eventually abated, so it could also slow in developing countries. Rising wages at home could eventually reduce the incentive to emigrate. Thus economic development and modernization could lead to a rise and subsequent fall in emigration – commonly referred to as the 'migration hump'[12].

How rich do people have to become before they stay at home? Some estimates have been made based on the European experience. Between the 1960s and the 1980s many people were migrating from the poorer countries of the South to the richer economies of the North. Then as incomes increased in Southern Europe emigration tailed off. The turning point in this case seemed to be an average per capita income of around $4,000 per year (in 1985 dollars). This is illustrated in figure 6.2 which shows how higher incomes first increased the likelihood of short-term migration such as that for seasonal agricultural work. Then it increased the possibilities for higher-cost, long-distance, unskilled migration and finally for higher skilled emigration. But when per capita income reached around $7,000 the impetus for large-scale emigration had substantially reduced. Since then, the critical income levels have probably increased – Mexico's per capita income is already over $7,000 – but the same principles should apply.

One crucial difference that developing countries face today, however, is a much more unstable economic environment. The huge flows of speculative capital washing around the world make it difficult to

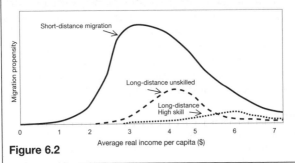

Fischer, P. and Straubhaar, T., 1996

The migration hump

When their countries start to industrialize, people's incomes and aspirations rise and they become more mobile and prone to emigrate. But as national average per capita incomes rise above $4,000, more opportunities open up at home and people feel less need to travel. This results in a 'migration hump', which is evident first for short-distance unskilled migrants and later for the more skilled workers. ■

Short-distance migration

Long-distance unskilled

Long-distance High skill

Migration propensity

Average real income per capita ($)

Figure 6.2

promote sustained economic development. In addition to the flows of investment funds indicated in figure 6.1 (p. 125) there are also massive speculative transfers on the foreign exchange markets. International currency dealers are currently handling around $1.3 trillion each day and can choose to attack the currency of any country, sending it on a rapid downward spiral. The ensuing crisis then triggers emigration. As a result of the 1995 peso crisis in Mexico, for example, the Mexican-US wage gap rose from around 8:1 to 12:1 and many more migrants headed for the border[13]. Similarly the Asian economic crisis in 1997 triggered sudden migrant flows in many directions: Thailand and Malaysia tried to expel foreign workers, while desperate Indonesians took the boats trying to find work overseas. The ongoing process of modernization compounded by the shocks delivered by globalization thus shakes more people loose from their familiar surroundings and opens up the prospect of emigration. Should globalization not be tamed the picture could turn much darker. Rather than going over a migration hump there is a danger that many countries could become stuck on the upward slope – with millions of young people angry and alienated, and all too aware that life could be much better elsewhere.

Just as the supply of migrants is likely to increase, so too is the demand. There is little evidence that people in the richer countries are prepared to do the kind of work that immigrants do. Indeed more and more jobs are being classified as suitable for immigrants. And given the ageing of the populations in the richer countries, there will be more calls for immigrants to provide medical and other care services.

Sane migration policies

For all the debate over globalization, there have been few efforts to address these new circumstances. We appear to have the worst of all worlds. The financial markets are out of control and capable of knocking even the most stable economies off balance. The international trade system is warped in favor of transnational corporations – so creates fewer opportunities for developing countries. Worst of all, the rich countries are tempting millions of people to travel and work illegally.

At present the governments of most rich countries shy away from equitable regulation of trade, finance, or migration. Instead they leave it to some of the world's poorest people to take the strain. International migrants have become the shock absorbers of the global economy, forced to embark on perilous voyages and to work illegally – and thus exposed to all forms of abuse and exploitation. In the United States the Immigration and Naturalization Service (INS) spends $2 billion each year in a high-profile defense of the border with Mexico. Yet the same agency makes little effort to police the enterprises who use immigrant workers. Indeed when the US economy is booming the number of apprehensions within the country drops noticeably. The INS knows that these workers are needed and that it would be very unpopular if it made serious efforts to clamp down on immigrant employment. US immigration policy thus criminalizes millions of people – employers and workers alike. Over half of the 1.6 million US farm workers are employed illegally[14].

The situation is no better in Europe. The south-western frontier outpost of 'Fortress Europe' is now Spain where around 50,000 illegal immigrants arrive each year. Many stay in Spain, doing the back-breaking work in the 10,000 hothouses that grow winter vegetables, or in the orange and olive groves of Andalusia, or in the factories of Barcelona. Others travel on to take similar jobs in France, or Germany, or the Netherlands. But many do not even survive the treacherous crossing from North Africa. The Moroccan Workers' Association in Spain estimates that between 1995 and 2000 around 3,000 people may have drowned. Probably the most horrific outcome of European defensive barriers, however, was in June 2000 when 58 Chinese immigrants suffocated to death in a container, attempting to enter the UK. The port of Dover is now notorious as the site of one of the world's worst migration tragedies.

Apart from the dangers they face trying to pierce border defenses, immigrants must then endure the hazards of working illegally. Employers who are confident that illegal workers will not be able to complain will often pay very low wages: US supermarkets, for example, can be paying illegal immigrants $3 an hour, compared with the statutory minimum wage of $5.15 an hour[15].

Undocumented immigrants in many industries are also exposed to dangerous working conditions or other forms of abuse. Women who have used Chinese snakeheads to smuggle them will often suffer physical and sexual assaults when they are kept in 'safe houses' where they are effectively imprisoned until they have paid off their fare.

Added to the this is the prospect of racial abuse and discrimination from the population at large. This can happen in all sorts of ways. In Rome, many advertisements for apartments explicitly exclude *stranieri*, 'foreigners'. At the other end of the extreme is the neo-Nazi racial violence meted out to immigrants in Germany and other European countries. Illegal immigrants are not of course alone in facing racial discrimination but they stand very little chance of redress.

If anything, political leaders have been making matters worse. As a sop to popular prejudice and the tabloid press they stir up animosity towards 'bogus asylum-seekers' and 'economic refugees' – throwing further fuel onto the fire. In January 2001 the Australian government took the process one stage further by using anti-immigrant sentiment as a way to dissuade immigrants. Officials prepared a kit of materials to be distributed to migrant-sending countries in the Middle East, warning that immigrants 'face racial hatred and violence because citizens are angry at having to support them.'[16]

Much of the abuse directed at immigrants results from a failure of government leadership. Few politicians are prepared to acknowledge the contribution of immigrants. Faced with a contradiction of real demand for workers on the one hand, and the political unpopularity of admitting more people on the other, they prefer to stand back and let the market decide, leaving immigrants to pay the price, if necessary with their lives.

Thus far the sacred texts of globalization, from NAFTA to the establishment of the World Trade Organization, have been strangely silent on the issue of migration. And calls for a United Nations conference on migration seem to have fallen on deaf ears. At the very least, governments need to make more realistic appraisals of their future needs for workers, and to cooperate with the sending countries to ensure that international migration is rational, regulated – and humane.

1 Williamson, J. 1996. 'Globalization, convergence, and history', in *The Journal of Economic History*, Vol. 56, No. 2. 2 Federici, N. (1989). 'Causes of international migration', in *The Impact of International Migration on Developing Countries*, Paris, OECD. 3 Pritchett, L. 1996. 'Forget convergence: Divergence past, present, and future', in *Finance and Development*, June. 4 UNDP, 1996. *Human Development Report*, New York, Oxford University Press. 5 Ward, R. (2001). 'Winners and losers' in *Economist*, April 28. 6 IMF/World Bank (2001). *Market Access for Developing Countries' Exports*, paper prepared by the Staffs of the IMF and the World Bank. www.worldbank.org/economics/marketaccess.pdf 7 Stalker, P. (1994). *The Work of Strangers*, Geneva, ILO. p. 158. 8 Martin, P. and Taylor, J. (1995). *Managing Migration: The Role of Economic Policies*, paper presented at the Migration Policy in Global Perspective conference at the New School, New York. 9 Economist (2001). 'Back office to the world', in *Economist*, May 3. 10 UNCTAD (2000). *World Investment Report*, Geneva. 11 UNCTAD (2000). Op. cit. 12 Martin, P. and Taylor, J. 1996. 'The anatomy of a migration hump', in *Development Strategies, Employment and Migration: Insights from Models*, Paris, OECD. 13 *Migration News* (1995), Volume 2, No. 4, April 14 De Palma, A. (2000). 'Farmers caught in conflict over illegal migrant workers', in *New York Times*, October 3. 15 Greenhouse, S. (2000). 'Foreign workers at highest level in seven decades', in *New York Times*, September 4. 16 Christie, M. (2001). 'Australia warns illegals of perils of migration'. Sydney, Reuters, January 10.

CONTACTS

International

International Organization for Migration
17 Route des Morillons, C.P. 71,
CH-1211, Geneva 19, Switzerland.
Tel: +41 22 717 9111
Fax: +41 22 798 6150
Email: info@iom.int
Website: www.iom.int

International Labour Organization (ILO)
4, Route des Morillons, CH-1211,
Geneva 22, Switzerland.
Tel: +41 22 799 6111
Fax: +41 22 798 8685
Email: ilo@ilo.org
Website: www.ilo.org

Migrant Rights International
Case postale 135, CH - 1211
Geneva 20, Switzerland.
Tel: +41 22 917 7817
Fax: +41 22 917 7810
Email: migrantwatch@vtx.ch
Website: www.migrantsrights.org

United Nations High Commissioner for Refugees (UNHCR)
C.P. 2500, 1211 Geneva 2, Switzerland.
Tel: +41 22 739 8111
Fax: +41 22 739 7314/15/16
Email: hqpi00@unhcr.ch
Website: www.unhcr.ch

Aotearaoa/New Zealand

Refugee & Migrant service
P O Box 11236, Manners Street,
Wellington.
Tel: +64 4 471 1932
Fax: +64 4 471 1938
Email: rms@actrix.gen.nz

Refugee & Migrant Centre
P O Box 13380, Christchurch.
Tel: +64 3 372 9310
Fax: +64 3 372 1310
E-mail: peetosch@ihug.co.nz

Australia

Federation of Ethnic Communities' Councils
PO Box 344, Curtin, ACT 2605.
(mailing address)
FECCA House, 1/4 Phipps Close,
Deakin, ACT 2600.
Tel: +61 2 6282 5755
Fax: +61 2 6282 5734
Email: feccadmin@fecca.org.au
Website: www.fecca.org.au

Refugee Council of Australia
PO Box 946, Glebe, 2037 NSW.
Tel: +61 2 9660 5300
Fax: +61 2 9660 5211
Email: rcoa@cia.com.au
Website: www.refugeecouncil.org.au

Canada

Canadian Ethnocultural Council
176 rue Gloucester St, Suite 400,
Ottawa, Ontario K2P 0A6.
Tel: +1 613 230 3867
Fax: +1 613 230 8051
Email: cec@web.net
Website: www.ethnocultural.ca

Canadian Council for Refugees
6839 Drolet #302, Montréal,
Québec, H2S 2T1.
Tel: +1 514 277 7223
Fax: +1 514 277 1447
Email: ccr@web.net
Website: www.web.net/~ccr/

Ontario Council of Agencies Serving Immigrants
110 Eglinton Ave. W. Suite 200,
Toronto, Ontario, M4R 1A3.
Tel: +1 416 322 4950
Fax: +1 416 322 8084
Email: generalmail@ocasi.org
Website: www.ocasi.org

Metropolitan Immigrant Settlement Association
Suite 200 2131 Gottingen St,
Halifax, NS B3K 5Z7.
Tel: +1 902 423 3607
Fax: +1 902 423 3154
E-mail: info@misa.ns.ca
Website: www.misa.ns.ca

UK

Greater Manchester Immigration Aid Unit
400 Cheetham Hill Road,
Manchester, M8 9LE.
Tel: +44 161 740 7722
Fax: +44 161 740 5172
Email: gmiau@mcr1.poptel.org.uk
Website: www.ein.org.uk/gmiau

Joint Council for the Welfare of Immigrants
115 Old Street, London EC1V 9RT.
Tel: +44 20 7251 8708
Fax: + 44 20 725 8707
Email: info@jcwi.org.uk
Website: www.jcwi.org.uk

Immigration Advisory Service
County House, 190 Great Dover Street. London SE1 4YB.
Tel: +44 20 7357 6917
Website: www.iasuk.org

Migrants Resource Center
24 Churton Street, London SW1V 2LP.
Tel: +44 20 7834 2505
Fax: +44 20 7931 8187
Email: migrantrc@gn.apc.org

National Coalition of Anti-deportation Campaigns
110 Hamstead Road,
Handsworth, Birmingham B20 2QS.
Tel: +44 121 554 6947
Fax: +44 121 055 4570
Email: ncadc@ncadc.org.uk
Website: www.ncadc.org.uk

Refugee Council
3 Bondway, London SW8 1SJ.
Tel: +44 20 7820 3000
Fax: +44 20 7582 9929
Email: info@refugeecouncil.org.uk
Wesbsite: www.refugeecouncil.org.uk

Stonewall Immigration Group
c/o Central Station, 37 Wharfdale Road, Islington, London N1 9SE.
Tel: +44 20 7713 0620
Email: info@stonewall-immigration.org.uk
Website: www.stonewall-immigration.org.uk

United States

National Network for Immigrant and Refugee Rights
310 8th Street, Suite 307, Oakland, CA 94607.
Tel: +1 510 465 1984
Fax: +1 510 465 1885
Email: nnirr@nnirr.org
Website: www.nnirr.org

Sweatshop Watch
310 8th Street, Suite 309, Oakland, CA 94607.
Tel: +1 510 834 8990
Email: sweatwatch@igc.org
Website: www.sweatshopwatch.org

Bibliography

Books

Detailed references are given at the end of each chapter. The following are some recent publications on international migration.

Guests and Aliens, Saskia Sassen (New Press, New York, 1999).

Open Borders: The Case against Immigration Controls, Teresa Hayter (Pluto Press, London, 2000).

Trends in International Migration. SOPEMI, (OECD, Paris, 2000).

World Migration Report 2000, International Organization for Migration, (IOM/UN, Geneva, 2000).

Workers Without Frontiers: The Impact of Globalization on International Migration, Peter Stalker (Lynne Rienner/ILO, Boulder Co, 2000).

Internet Resources

There are now thousands of websites covering international migration. Some useful starting points are:

December 18 – A global portal run by an international network of volunteers and NGOs for the promotion and protection of the rights of migrants. www.december18.net

Electronic Immigration Network – Based in the UK but with many international links. www.ein.org.uk

Immigration Index – A clear and comprehensive directory of migration links. www.immigrationindex.org.

Migration News – Based in the United States at the University of California, Davis. A comprehensive up-to-date digest of international migration information, compiled monthly from the world's media. Part of the Migration Dialogue site. http://migration.ucdavis.edu/mn.

Scalabrini Migration Center – Based in the Philippines. Good coverage of Asian migration issues, including Asian Migration News. www.scalabrini.org/~smc/

WWW Virtual Library on Migration and Ethnic Relations – A useful starting point, though weighted towards academic links. www.ercomer.org/wwwvl.

Index

Index

Index

Index

Index